IC & BITTERS

VERMOUTHS

CH SPIRITS

GIN

LE GIN

CRAFT DISTILLING

THE SPIRIT OF GIN

Also by Matt Teacher:

The Home Distiller's Handbook: Make Your Own Whiskey & Bourbon Blends, Infused Spirits and Cordials (Cider Mill Press, 2011)

The Little Pink Book of Cocktails (Cider Mill Press, 2009)

THE SPIRIT OF

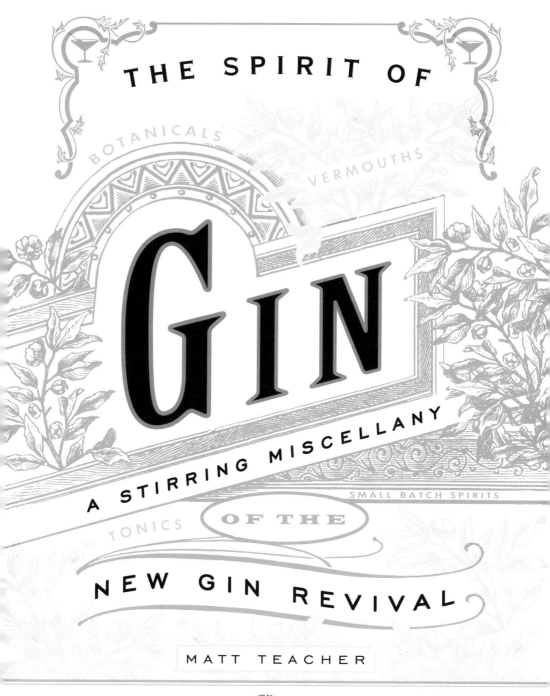

BOTANICALS

VERMOUTHS

GIN

A STIRRING MISCELLANY

TONICS OF THE

SMALL BATCH SPIRITS

NEW GIN REVIVAL

MATT TEACHER

CIDER MILL PRESS BOOK PUBLISHERS
KENNEBUNKPORT, MAINE

Visit us on the Web!
www.cidermillpress.com

Cover design by Whitney Cookman
Interior design by Alicia Freile, Tango Media
Illustrations: Sherry Berger
Typography: Algerian, Birka, Chevalier Stripes, and Whitney

Printed in China

2 3 4 5 6 7 8 9 0

This book is dedicated to Mary Ann, Richie, Buz, Janet, Benny and Katie. Thank you for your never-ending love and support.

CONTENTS

COCKTAIL RECIPES

FOREWORD

In the beginning there was gin, whiskey, rum, and cognac.
And these four things were never to be mixed together.

Then came other things, such as vermouth, sweet liqueurs, sugar, and lemon,
which were created to serve the greater glory of the first four elements of the world.

On the sixth day, God created the Barman. Instead of Eve, He gave him
a shaker, then ice, and then a couple of glasses.

And He said:
"Mix for the joy of your neighbors."

My father, Giuseppe, was born in Verona, the son of an immigrant, the late Carlo. In 1929 my father was working as a barman at the Hotel Europa in Venice. One of his disciples was a young American named Harry. Harry was very rich, but to our great good fortune he did not have a credit card—it was one of the things that hadn't yet been invented. If there had been credit cards in 1929, there never would have been Harry's Bar. I'll tell you why.

One day young Harry ran out of money and my father lent him an amount to cover the hotel bill, the sizable bar tab, and the cost of the ticket to travel back to his home in Boston.

Two years later, Harry Pickering, that was his family name, returned to Venice to pay my father's loan back. On top of that, he also offered an extra amount to become partners in a new venture, a bar, which they both agreed had to be called "Harry's Bar."

I love gin. *Gin and Tonic* is the name of my boat and of my house in Punta del Este.

I am not very keen on vodka. Gin has never deceived me. Vodka did; at least once. One evening I had dinner at Harry's Bar with a few friends. I don't remember why, but we all drank vodka martinis. As I was trying to walk back home, I fell on the last bridge before my Venetian shelter. As it often miraculously happens to people who had too much to drink, I did not get hurt. But something else happened. The next morning my wife told me that as I saw her waiting, I asked her quite solemnly if she would marry me. I had forgotten that I had already married her 55 years before!

It never would have happened with gin.

This book is a jewel and a must-read for anyone who knows gin and loves it. We all have to thank Matt Teacher for having done it with dedication, love, and competence.

I am only 82 years old and I sincerely believe that gin is one of the great gifts that helps us get through the asperity of happenings with the proper lightness and a noble attitude.

Gin is luxury. Luxury is to be alive.

—*Arrigo Cipriani, Venice, Italy, 2014*

INTRODUCTION

I embarked on my research for this book as a gin enthusiast, appreciator and consumer with a common knowledge of its place in the world of spirits. I could not have dreamt that the story and journey that lay before me would hold such history and evolution, innovative wizard-minds and age-old wisdom, hard-cut facts and mythical legends, tradition and innovation. The spirit we call gin has, within it, an intricate societal role that is still unraveling today. At the moment, we are riding the wave of a new gin revival thanks to a remarkable number of new producers—as well as established distillers—who have introduced a wide range of unusual botanicals to create stunning new flavor profiles. The journey is not over, and the adventure has only begun.

The Rival Majicians [sic] or Raising the Spirit, *published in* The Satarist [sic] in England (1808).

From the first written mention of the juniper-flavored spirit "genever" (or "jenever") in the Middle Ages, when it became popular in the Lowlands of present-day Belgium and the Netherlands for its purported medicinal qualities, to the London Gin Craze in the first half of the eighteenth century where the public and Parliament battled to find a balance between life and law, to today, the juniper berry has been there. From the juice of gluttons to James Bond's lips, gin has seen its cultural status fluctuate within the tides of history.

Today we have the luxury of riding a growing surge of interest in all things local and craft. From coffee to jewelry and many things in between,

the closer the source and the more natural the formula, the wider the appeal—and perhaps the better for you, as well as for your local economy. Gin is no exception.

Improvisation is what moves the tides of innovation and progress, popular taste, and, in plush times, a drive for something more. As our world begins the twenty-first century, gin, once again, has tiptoed out of the shadows and into our glasses in growing numbers. After I had the privilege of chatting up gin authorities around the world and discussing the products they produce and the cocktails they craft, one thing became clear—different ingredients and atmospheres produce different results.

The climate of the United States is much different than that of England; a different set of locally grown ingredients is available and therefore the products are distinctive. Brooklyn's Greenhook Ginsmiths has produced Beach Plum Gin Liqueur, a modern American take on a sloe gin, crafted in the absence of fresh sloe berries yet delivering an accurate representation, along with its own unique perfection. Sloe berries don't cultivate on United States soil and to ship them in a timely, unspoiled fashion is not possible.

If a distiller can source local botanicals for their gins, it becomes unique to their locale and also promotes the modern farm-to-table ideology. Vermont's Caledonia Spirits, for example, produces Barr Hill gin made with its own farmed honey. Similar stories of local flavor abound in today's gin scene.

Above: Lucas Bols genever bottles from the 1600s to modern times.
Left: Juniper berries.

My travels for this book have taken me from predictable rainy days in London, England, to the cool breezes of Portland, Oregon; from 98-degree hikes through Brooklyn, New York, to a sunny-day stroll to Harry's Bar in Venice, Italy; and to other points and people of interest in between. I was provoked to continue chasing the story—having discovered that each bar, each cocktail-crafter, and each experience was remarkably different—and I became connected to a network of places and personalities, communities and partnerships, that thrived on their cooperation and uniqueness. They didn't all agree, but I must admit, they all loved gin, and all had an understanding and appreciation that they so kindly imparted—along with dozens of their craft cocktail recipes you'll find inside. I'm appreciative of everyone I met and connected with during this adventure, and I am pleased to add their knowledge and experience to this book.

Bar Hill Gin epitomizes the current farm-to-table attitude by using their own homemade honey in the distillation process.

Vintage Lucas Bols ad.

THE LONDON GIN CLUB

THE STAR AT NIGHT
22 GREAT CHAPEL STREET
SOHO, LONDON, ENGLAND
WWW.THELONDONGINCLUB.COM

L ondon is an amazing yet foreign place to me. The city spoke such a familiar, and at the same time completely different, language from my hometown of Philadelphia. While I had not set foot on the European continent until I began researching this book, I did know that if there was one place a person interested in gin must visit, it was England. They had all the early history. As I asked fellow cocktail appreciators where I must go and whom I must meet while in London, one person and venue kept coming up—Julia Forte at the London Gin Club. So I contacted Julia, the

proprietor of the Star at Night, a venue that has been in her family for generations and from which she launched the Gin Club. Julia was kind enough to invite me (along with my father) to meet her at the club and discuss the state of gin in London.

At the end of a side street in the Soho district, a sign hangs— not for the London Gin Club but for the Star at Night. Those in the know can confidently walk in after six in the evening, any Monday through Thursday,

The London Gin Club serves cocktails in balloon glasses to enhance the sensory experience.

and expect to find the Gin Club in progress. Old advertising signs adorn the wooden walls as overhead lighting illuminates seating for the guests. Behind the wooden bar, open-faced cabinets are stocked three or four gin bottles deep. Like looking at the ocean, I was only seeing the surface.

If you like gin, this is the place to be. I ask Julia what someone joining the Gin Club should expect. She answers, "They will experience probably the best gin and tonic they've had. Not only being served in the balloon glass, which is ice chilled with a specifically paired garnish, but also we crack our own large blocks of ice which is twice frozen to ensure the drink stays cold and not water-diluted. We always serve single-

Chile, Basil & Cucumber 'Ginfusion'

4 oz. gin
2 slices chile
1 sprig basil
2 slices cucumber

Muddle all three ingredients in a glass with gin. Strain over ice and top with tonic.

pour tonics, from glass bottles, so it's crisp, cold and sparkling. Every element of a G&T is important and we choose the best for each element. Plus, we're friendly, a little bit obsessive about what we do, so you won't get a better gin experience here in London!"

I ask Julia why she chose to serve her cocktails in balloon glasses, a practice I had never seen in the States. Julia tells me, "We serve our gin and tonics in a balloon serve or copa glass. This glass does to gin what a wine glass does to red wine; it allows the flavor to come out, and only in a copa glass do you really experience the true flavors of gin."

My eyes wander left toward the wooden cabinets housing the bottles of gin, some so mysterious to me I have to restrain myself from walking behind the bar to pick one up, just to hold and look at it. We stand up and walk over to the bar. As the man who introduced me to the pure joy of a martini, I am grateful that my dad is here. From behind the bar Julia proceeds to show us various bottles neither of us had ever seen before, including the elusive Monkey 47 German gin, and describes how each one pairs with garnishes differently. That is not a distinction usually made in the United States (just throw a lime on the side!). I ask Julia to elaborate on how she pairs specific garnishes with gins based on their flavor profile. Julia explains, "We look at each gin and

Cardamon & Orange Gimlet

2 oz. single-distillate cardamom gin
1 oz. fresh orange juice
1 oz. fresh lime juice
1 oz. sugar syrup*
Fresh cardamoms

Combine all ingredients in a shaker. Shake and serve straight in a martini glass. (*Sugar syrup: 1 part sugar, 1 part water.)

Ginger Tom

2 oz. London dry gin
1 oz. King's ginger liqueur
½ oz. fresh lemon juice
½ oz. sugar syrup*

Combine gin, sugar syrup and lemon juice in a Collins glass over cracked ice and stir. Top with King's ginger liqueur. (*Sugar syrup: 1 part sugar, 1 part water.)

Gatsby-Style Raspberry Rickey

2 oz. gin
2 oz. lime juice
1 oz. sugar syrup*
5 raspberries
1 oz. soda water
1 lime peel

Combine gin, lime juice, sugar syrup and raspberries in a shaker with ice. Shake and strain over ice and top with soda. Garnish with raspberries and lime peel. (*Sugar syrup: 1 part sugar, 1 part water.)

establish what is the main or leading botanical. We then either pair with this or contrast with this to bring its flavor out. For example, rhubarb, lime and olive work well to bring up the flavor of juniper. Rose enhances saffron. Coriander or a savory garnish will lift and show off a sweet gin."

There is only one item on the menu that is not mouthwatering, so to speak, and that is the London Gin Club's brilliantly conceived *Underground Map of Gin*, featuring "All the gin facts you'll ever need." (See the copy that Julia gifted to me on page 22). We didn't taste any gin in this meeting, but I believe both our curiosities left thirstier than ever. The London Gin Club has an active web presence that provides a lot of valuable information. I highly recommend looking to the club for breaking news on the latest gins, unique gin experiences, and gin history.

"We're friendly, a little bit obsessive about what we do, so you won't get a better gin experience here in London!"

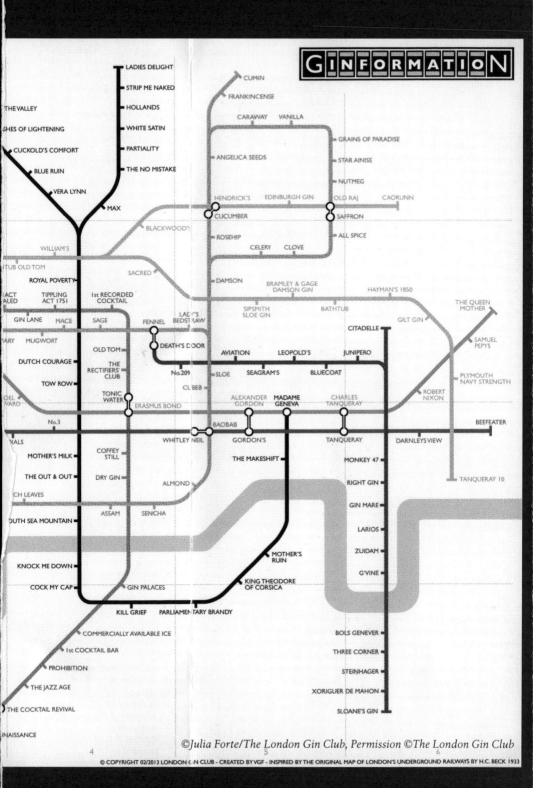

GINFORMATION

LADIES DELIGHT · STRIP ME NAKED · HOLLANDS · WHITE SATIN · PARTIALITY · THE NO MISTAKE

CUMIN · FRANKINCENSE · CARAWAY · VANILLA · GRAINS OF PARADISE · STAR AINISE · NUTMEG

THE VALLEY · SHES OF LIGHTENING · CUCKOLD'S COMFORT · BLUE RUIN · VERA LYNN · MAX

ANGELICA SEEDS · HENDRICK'S · EDINBURGH GIN · OLD RAJ · CAORUNN

BLACKWOOD'S · CUCUMBER · SAFFRON

WILLIAM'S · ROSEHIP · ALL SPICE · CELERY · CLOVE

TUB OLD TOM · SACRED · ROYAL POVERTY · DAMSON · BRAMLEY & GAGE DAMSON GIN · HAYMAN'S 1850

ACT ALED · TIPPLING ACT 1751 · 1st RECORDED COCKTAIL · SIPSMITH SLOE GIN · BATHTUB · THE QUEEN MOTHER

GIN LANE · MACE · SAGE · FENNEL · LADY'S BEDSTRAW · GILT GIN · SAMUEL PEPYS

MARY · MUGWORT · OLD TOM · DEATH'S DOOR · AVIATION · LEOPOLD'S · JUNIPERO · CITADELLE

DUTCH COURAGE · THE RECTIFIERS' CLUB · No.209 · SLOE · SEAGRAM'S · BLUECOAT · PLYMOUTH NAVY STRENGTH

TOW ROW · CUBEB · ROBERT NIXON

OEL WARD · TONIC WATER · ERASMUS BOND · ALEXANDER GORDON · MADAME GENEVA · CHARLES TANQUERAY

No.3 · BAOBAB · BEEFEATER

DIALS · WHITLEY NEIL · GORDON'S · TANQUERAY · DARNLEYS VIEW

MOTHER'S MILK · COFFEY STILL · THE MAKESHIFT · MONKEY 47

THE OUT & OUT · DRY GIN · RIGHT GIN · TANQUERAY 10

CH LEAVES · ALMOND · GIN MARE

OUTH SEA MOUNTAIN · ASSAM · SENCHA · LARIOS

ZUIDAM

KNOCK ME DOWN · MOTHER'S RUIN · G'VINE

COCK MY CAP · GIN PALACES · KING THEODORE OF CORSICA

KILL GRIEF · PARLIAMENTARY BRANDY

COMMERCIALLY AVAILABLE ICE · BOLS GENEVER

1st COCKTAIL BAR · THREE CORNER

PROHIBITION · STEINHAGER

THE JAZZ AGE · XORIGUER DE MAHON

THE COCKTAIL REVIVAL · SLOANE'S GIN

NAISSANCE

©Julia Forte/The London Gin Club, Permission ©The London Gin Club

4 · 5 · 6

A

RICK BLAINE

WINSTON SMITH

THE QUEEN

CHARLES DICKENS

ORSON WELLS   BOB HOPE   MRS BEETON

F. SCOTT FITZGERALD   ERNEST HEMINGWAY   W.C. FIELDS

GIN FIZZ

BEE'S KNEES

WHITE LADY

WILLIAM OF ORANGE

AQUA VITAE

JUNIPER EAU DE VIE

DUTCH GENEVER

30 YEARS WAR

WORSHIPFUL COMPANY OF DISTILLERS

DISTILLING ACT 1690

DRAM SHOPS

BRIEF HISTORY OF DISTILLERS

CREAM OI

FLA

OXLEY

BOMBAY ORIGINAL

PORTOBELLO ROAD

LONDON No.1

BROKERS

GRAPEFRUIT

LEMON

TANQUERAY RANGPUR

GIN RICKEY

DANIEL DEFOE

GIN CRAZE

GIN RIOTS

BOMBAY SAPPHIRE   ADNAM'S FIRST RATE   BRECON

BOTANIST

GIN ACT 1736

BATH

SIR JOSEPH JEKYLL

PUSS & MEOW

GIN REPR

B

RANGPUR LIME

CLEMENTINE

BITTER ORANGE

POMELO

MARTINI

NEGRONI   FRENCH 75

Capt DUDLEY BRADSTREET

BOG MYRTLE   SAVORY   LEMONGRASS   WORMWOOD

HEATHER   MEADOW SWEET   MINT   THYME   ROSE

ISH

HAYMAN'S GIN LIQUEUR

CITY OF LONDON

LIME

JASMINE

CLOVER CLUB

HONEYSUCKLE

GIN & IT

WINSTON CHURCHILL

JOHN F. KENNEDY

HIBISCUS

GIN CRUSTA

N CO

COLONEL FOX   SW4

MARTIN MILLER'S   JENSON

OLD ENGLISH

SIPSMITH   BLOOM   GILPIN'S

GERANIUM   FIFTY POUNDS   BERKELEY SQUARE

HAYMAN'S LONDON DRY

BERGAMOT

SWEET ORANGE

ORANGE BLOSSOM

CREEPING THISTLE

RAMOS GIN FIZZ

C

SARSAPARILLA   BURDOCK

MARSHMALLOW   GINGER

6 O'CLOCK

LANGTONS No.1

OAK BARK

CINNAMON

PLYMOUTH

ROSE   LAVENDER   ELDERFLOWER

IRIS   CHAMOMILE   HAWTHORN   KAFFIR LIME

ANGELICA ROOT

ORRIS

CARDAMON

CASSIA BARK

MARTINEZ

PINK GIN

GIN SLING

SUMMER CUP

LICORICE

CORIANDER

JUNIPER

GIN SMASH

GIMLET

SOUTHSIDE

TOM COLLINS

THE G

D

OUTER LONDON LINE   HISTORY LINE
LONDON DRY LINE   PEOPLE LINE
INTERNATIONAL LINE   COCKTAILS LINE
BOTANICALS LINE   PSEUDONYM LINE

PLEASE DRINK RESPONSIBLY

1   2   3

UNDERGROUND
MAP OF GIN

A new design for an old map.
Issued by the London Gin Club.

All the Gin facts you'll ever need.

Issue No. 1   2013

GINDEX

1st COCKTAIL BAR
1st RECORDED COCKTAIL - B4
30 YEARS WAR - A2
6 O'CLOCK - C1
7 DIALS - C4
ADNAMS FIRST RATE - B2
ALEXANDER GORDON - C5
ALL SPICE - B5
ALMOND - B5
ANGELICA ROOT - C2
ANGELICA SEEDS - A5
AQUA VITAE - A2
ASSAM - C4
AVIATION - B5
BAOBAB - C5
BATHTUB - B5
BATHTUB OLD TOM - B4
BRAMLEY & GAGE DAMSON GIN - B5
BEEFEATER - C6
BEE'S KNEES - A2
BERGAMOT - C1
BERKELEY SQUARE - C3
BIRCH LEAVES - C4
BITTER ORANGE - B1
BLACKWOOD'S - B4
BLOOM - C2
BLUE COAT - B5
BLUE RUIN - A4
BOB HOPE - A1
BOG MYRTLE - B2
BOLS GENEVER - D6
BOMBAY ORIGINAL - B1
BOMBAY SAPPHIRE - B2
BOTANIST - B3
BRECON - B3
BRIEF HISTORY OF DISTILLERS - A3
BROKERS - B1
BURDOCK - C2
Capt. DUDLEY BRADSTREET - B3
CAORUNN - A6
CARAWAY - A5
CARDAMON - C2
CASSIA BARK - D2
CELERY - B5
CHAMOMILE - C2
CHARLES DICKENS - A1
CHARLES TANQUERAY - C5
CINNAMON - D1
CITADELLE - B6
CLEMENTINE - B1
CLOVER CLUB - B3
CLOVE - B5
COCK MY CAP - D4
COCKTAIL REVIVAL - D3
COFFEY STILL - C4
COMMERCIALLY AVAILABLE ICE - D4

COLONEL FOX - C1
CORIANDER - D2
CREAM OF THE VALLEY - A3
CREEPING THISTLE - C2
CUBEB - B5
CUCKOLD'S COMFORT - A4
CUCUMBER - A5
CUMIN - A5
DAMSON - B5
DANIEL DEFOE - B3
DARNLEY'S VIEW - C6
DEATH'S DOOR - B4
DISTILLING ACT 1690 - A2
DRAM SHOPS - A3
DRY GIN - C4
DUTCH COURAGE - B4
DUTCH GENEVER - A2
EDINBURGH GIN - A5
ERNEST HEMINGWAY - A2
ELDERFLOWER - C3
ERASMUS BOND - C4
F. SCOTT FITZGERALD - A2
FENNEL - B4
FIFTY POUNDS - C3
FLASHES OF LIGHTENING - A3
FRANKINCENSE - A5
FRENCH 75 - B2
G'VINE - C6
GERANIUM - C3
GILT GIN - B6
GILPIN'S - C3
GIN & IT - B3
GIN ACT 1736 - B3
GIN ACT REPEALED - A3
GIN CRAZE - B3
GIN CRUSTA - B3
GIN FIZZ - A2
GIN LANE - B4
GIN MARE - C6
GIN PALACES - D4
GIN RICKEY - A2
GIN RIOTS - B3
GIN SLING - C3
GIN SMASH - D3
GINGER - C2
GIMLET - C3
GINAISSANCE - D3
GRAINS OF PARADISE - A5
GRAPEFRUIT - B1
HAWTHORN - C3
HAYMAN'S 1850 - B6
HAYMAN'S LONDON DRY - C3
HAYMAN'S GIN LIQUEUR - B1
HEATHER - B2
HENDRICK'S - A5
HIBISCUS - C2
HOLLANDS - A4
HONEYSUCKLE - B2
IRIS - C2
ISH - B1

JASMINE - B2
JAZZ AGE - D4
JENSON - C1
JOHN F. KENNEDY - B3
JUNIPER - D2
JUNIPER EAU DE VIE - A2
JUNIPERO - B6
KAFFIR LIME - C3
KILL GREIF - D4
KING THEODORE OF CORSICA - C5
KNOCK ME DOWN - C4
LADIES DELIGHT - A4
LADY'S BEDSTRAW - B5
LANGTONS No.1 - C1
LARIOS - C6
LAVENDER - C3
LEMON - B1
LEMONGRASS - B3
LEOPOLD'S - B5
LICORICE - D2
LIME - C1
LONDON No.1 - B1
MACE - B4
MAKESHIFT - C5
MADAME GENEVA - C5
MARSHMALLOW - C2
MARTIN MILLER'S - C1
MARTINEZ - C3
MARTINI - B2
MAX - A4
MEADOW SWEET - B3
MINT - B3
MONKEY 47 - C6
MOTHER'S MILK - C4
MOTHER'S RUIN - C5
MRS BEETON - A1
MUGWORT - B4
NEGRONI - B2
No.209 - B5
No.3 - C4
NOEL COWARD - B4
NO MISTAKE - A4
NUTMEG - A5
OAK MARK - C1
OLD ENGLISH - C1
OLD RAJ - A5
OLD TOM - B4
ORANGE BLOSSOM - C2
ORRIS - C2
ORSON WELLS - A1
OUT & OUT - C4
OXLEY - A2
PARLIAMENTARY BRANDY - D5
PARTIALITY - A4
PINK GIN - C3
PLYMOUTH - D1
PLYMOUTH NAVY STRENGTH - B6
POMELO - B1
PORTOBELLO ROAD - B1
PROHIBITION - D4

PUSS & MEOW - B3
RAMOS GIN FIZZ - C3
RANGPUR LIME - B1
RECTIFIERS' CLUB - D4
RICK BLAINE - A1
RIGHT GIN - C6
ROBERT NIXON - B6
ROSE - C2
ROYAL POVERTY - B4
ROSEHIP - B5
ROSEMARY - B3
SACRED - B4
SAFFRON - A5
SAGE - B4
SAMUEL PEPYS - B6
SARSAPARILLA - C2
SAVORY - B3
SEAGRAMS - B5
SENCHA - C4
SIPSMITH - C2
SIPSMITH SLOE GIN - B5
SIR JOSEPH JEKYLL - B3
SLOANE'S GIN - D6
SLOE - B5
SOUTH SEA MOUNTAIN - C4
SOUTHSIDE - D3
STEINHAGER - D6
STRIP ME NAKED - A4
STAR ANISE - A5
SUMMER CUP - D3
SW4 - C1
SWEET ORANGE - C1
TANQUERAY - C5
TANQUERAY 10 - C6
TANQUERAY RANGPUR
THE QUEEN - A1
THE QUEEN MOTHER - B6
THREE CORNER - D6
THYME - B3
TIPPLING ACT 1751 - B4
TOM COLLINS - D3
TONIC WATER - B4
TOW ROW - B4
VANILLA - A5
VERA LYNN - A4
WILLIAM'S - B4
W.C. FIELDS - A2
WHITE LADY
WHITE SATIN - A4
WHITLEY NEIL - C5
WILLIAM OF ORANGE - A2
WILLIAM'S - B4
WINSTON CHURCHILL - B3
WINSTON SMITH - A1
WORMWOOD - B3
WORSHIPFUL Co. OF DISTILLERS - A2
XORIGUER DE MAHON - D6
ZUIDAM - C6

On the Gatefold: A reproduction of the London Gin Club's ingenious Ginformation map.

A HISTORICAL ACCOUNT of GIN

The oral and written record of "Madame Geneva"—an eighteenth century British sobriquet for gin—expresses a unique angle on history. Looking back to periods where alcohol, and gin specifically, played a key role in society gives us an understanding and appreciation for the ever-enduring spirit of gin. Its tale captures movements in time where political, religious, moral, and aristocratic presences turned the world in new directions.

Gin's epitaph would be lengthy and full of moments of praise and celebration, intoxication and condemnation, sophisticated encounters and severe moral disdain. Yet despite its setbacks over time, gin is not dead. In fact, gin is more alive than ever. By observing a few significant historical periods and events in both London and America, we can better understand where gin's image came from and where it is going today.

Were the periods of the London Gin Craze and US Prohibition all that different? Although the details vary and two centuries lay between them, the public reaction, social outcomes, and eventual regress connect these two

Federal agents destroy a barrel of alcohol during US Prohibition.
Overleaf: The boiler in a small Old Country gin distillery.

eras together. If the United States had looked to early eighteenth-century London as a case study, perhaps Prohibition—which fueled the growth of organized crime and underground markets while simultaneously forfeiting the government's tax revenue from spirits—would have been rethought. Today many forward thinkers, typically not those in politics or the for-profit prison system, make the association between Prohibition and the current "War on Drugs" the United States has pursued fruitlessly for decades. Can a government effectively regulate what substances its citizens ingest?

Within the last decade, the upswing of gin producers has grown exponentially, and like any other growth market, it can be attributed first to one factor—demand. The popularity of gin in countries such as Spain, Germany, and the United States continues to rise as new distilleries release exceptional gin labels and new bars open their doors with a focus on gin cocktails and selection. For a lover of gin, this is a good time to be alive.

THE LONDON GIN CRAZE

As Great Britain barreled into the eighteenth century, many factors— political, social and economic—set the scene for what would become one of gin's darker historical moments. Today, looking back in time and across the Atlantic from the United States, it seems as if gin, although unequivocally a dynamic factor, became a scapegoat and took all the blame for society's ills. And like so many morally motivated political moves, those who thought they knew what was best for others ended up conjuring the very things they sought to avoid.

While London was home to a sufficient population of well-to-dos, there also existed, particularly in the East End and West End neighborhoods, communities fueled by poverty, criminal activity, and the manic fear of the spreading bubonic plague. Unrest, a desperate need to escape a harsh reality, and the potential to make a penny were all tensions building amongst the impoverished.

Greed Leads to Gluttony

In 1690 land-owning aristocrats, anxious to keep the value of grain up so that their land rents would sustain, passed "An Act for the Encouraging of the Distillation of Brandy and Spirits from Corn." This act produced a surge in gin production and consumption, based on several factors:

- Simultaneously lowered the duty on malted corn distillates while raising the tax on beer and spirits made from other sources
- Placed a more severe duty on spirits imported from France
- Allowed an eager distiller, with little capital, to pay a small fee for a license and begin production within ten days

This first act, which was spectacularly successful in increasing landowners' revenues and Britain's collected duties, set into motion a course that, despite a series of licit attempted remedies, would upset England over the next half century. If this first act had been left alone, perhaps the Gin Craze would not be so notorious today. That is not to say that production and consumption did not rise drastically after the act's implementation, but those who morally objected to the spirit did not do themselves any favors as they attempted to regulate gin's consumption.

The thirst for gin seemed to have no bounds, and by 1716 gin was being served in all manner of establishments and street-carts that were frequented by London's budding urban populace of over half a million. Enabled by easy access to distilling permits, many adaptations on what was previously considered "gin" appeared, and not for the better. Gin was being produced by large distilleries, small independents, and in the criminal shadows. Traditionally, juniper berries had to be procured, dried and prepared before making a gin. That took too much time and effort for some fervent smaller distillers. Instead they tried, with varying amounts of success, to imitate juniper's essence using a combination of lesser-quality additives and flavorings, including oil of turpentine, oil of almonds, pepper, ginger and sulfuric acid. Often the harsh taste would be cut with sugar in order to make it more palatable. Certainly some of these concoctions would not even be considered gin today.

Many people—including women, for the first time in history—were frequently seen intoxicated in public, and the streets bustled with mischief, gluttony and prostitution. Rumors and stories began circulating about

The Gin Shop *from the series* The Drunkard's Children, *by George Cruikshank (1848).*

mothers forgetting to feed their babies, men getting into violent fights in the street, and criminals waiting in the alleys for their next target. All this was attributed to the abundance of gin.

ATTEMPTS AT REFORMATION—THE GIN ACTS

The Society for the Reformation of Manners—one of many similar socially conservative activist groups of the day—did not approve of what they witnessed. They considered gin to be a poison that resulted in loosened morals, criminal activity, and indecency, and they took political action to further their position. The society's first "success" came in 1729 when the first Gin Act was passed. This act attempted to tighten the nation's loose grip on spirits by more than doubling the duty and instating a permit fee for spirit retailers. This measure did not work.

Although there would soon be fewer distillers on the official books due to the associated fees, a surge in illegal bootlegging quickly took off and people were drinking more than ever. Just four years later, upon seeing what their actions had spurred, the act was repealed in 1733.

MAKE YOUR OWN GIN—LEGALLY!

Some say gin is like vodka with personality. In fact, some gin makers use vodka as their base spirit when making gin. Vodka may be seen as a cocktail artist's blank palette upon which the crafter may paint their desired botanical flavor profile.

Why not try your hand at crafting some of your own gin? There are kits available to help you do just that (www.homemadegin.com). You won't actually be distilling but rather infusing or macerating vodka or neutral grain alcohol (not included in the kit) with botanicals, including juniper and a container with a unique blend of spices, botanicals and flowers.

While gin-making kits typically come with botanicals, the adventurous may want to research and source their own spices and botanicals for experimentation. You can easily purchase juniper berries online at websites such as www.starwest-botanicals.com. A trip to your local market or Asian spice shop will provide you with a lot of other options for your palate.

Despite the Society for the Reformation of Manners' retracted effort, it did not take long for another morally minded group, the Society for Promoting Christian Knowledge, to decide it was their turn to invoke action. In search of a reformed London, the Gin Act of 1736 was passed. Acting as if they had not observed the actions of their predecessors, the authors of this act made it even more severe, raising the duty and license fees to levels that priced out those who wanted gin the most. The "death of gin" was subsequently mourned in public as mock funerals for Madame Geneva, held by crowds adorned in black, were staged in public protest.

Throughout history, attempting to push any manner of abstinence on the people rarely triumphs. In response to the 1736 Gin Act, the market plunged even deeper underground into less regulated, less responsible hands. The gin-drinking citizens of London, when faced with sobriety, became very creative to ensure the fate of gin was not doomed.

One notable figure, Dudley Bradstreet, was an imaginative entrepreneur. A man of many exploits, Bradstreet may be most recognized for his ingenious "Old Tom" cat scheme. In 1736, he had an associate discretely rent a house in London's Saint Luke's Parish with a business venture in mind. He purchased a painted sign depicting a cat with one paw extended, and nailed it over a window facing the street. Underneath the paw, Bradstreet hid a hollow pipe running to the house interior. In-the-know customers placed their coinage into the cat's mouth and whispered, "Puss, give me two pennies' worth of gin." After which they would hold their cup, or perhaps mouth, to the pipe and receive their juice. This inspired many imitators, and although profitable for Bradstreet, he soon closed in search of other ventures.

As Parliament tried to regain control of London, two more Gin Acts were instituted in 1737 and 1738. These acts amplified penalties for unlicensed vending and attempted to protect the informers who were relied on by the government to call out illegal activity. Again, looking back, it is clear that both of these acts only increased illegal production and consumption.

LESSONS ALMOST LEARNED

By 1743 the British political attitude once again turned. The reforms were only working *against* those who promoted them, and the sense of lost control became overwhelming. The 1743 Gin Act returned distilling permits to an obtainable price while still seeking to cash in on the duties from spirits. While there were some who remained diligent in their effort to completely ban gin, the act could be considered a success in terms of the stream of licenses sold and duties collected. As more licensed distilleries opened their doors, the need for illicit producers waned. Gin consumption was on the decline and things seemed to be leveling off. The battle was not over just yet, however.

THE RISE OF BRITISH NATIONAL SPIRIT CONSUMPTION

1684: 572,000 gallons
1700: 1,223,000 gallons
1710: 2,000,000 gallons

1730: 3,000,000 gallons
1735: 6,000,000 gallons
1743: 8,000,000 gallons

A BALANCE IS STRUCK

By 1748 the War of the Austrian Succession was over and eighty thousand British sailors and soldiers, many of whom had developed an inclination toward vice, were returning to London and other English cities. A fear of what would become of these new inhabitants weighed on many minds. Having observed a slow recovery since the Gin Act of 1743, elites were driven to take a preventative measure in an effort to stunt the potential for societal regression.

Whether through poetry or painting, song or sermon, the arts have both captured and skewed public perception with swift efficacy throughout history. In 1751 artist William Hogarth made two engravings, *Gin Lane* and *Beer Street*, which were published in the *London Evening-Post*. *Gin Lane* illustrates a chaotic city street featuring a bare-breasted drunken mother gazing down with a blank stare and smirk as her baby falls over the railing. All around is madness, death and violence. This image, in conjunction with an anti-gin pamphlet created and distributed by Westminster magistrate Henry Fielding, once again caused a social stir and rallied Parliament to take action. These men wanted nothing more than complete prohibition. Luckily, they would have to compromise.

Gin Lane *by William Hogarth (1751).*

Here is a transcription of the poem that appears at the bottom of the print *Gin Lane*, seen on the previous page:

Gin cursed Fiend, with Fury fraught,
Makes human Race a Prey.
It enters by a deadly Draught
And steals our Life away.

Virtue and Truth, driv'n to Despair,
It's Rage compells to fly,
But cherishes, with hellish Care,
Theft, Murder, Perjury.

Damned Cup! that on the Vitals preys,
That liquid Fire contains,
Which Madness to the Heart conveys,
And rolls it thro' the Veins.

With the Gin Act of 1751 Britain finally reached a balance between religious and moral groups, and society at large. Duties were raised, but not exorbitantly, and permits were accessible enough to deem illegal operations as futile. Gin was no longer the cheapest high, and the curtain closed on the London Gin Craze.

LONDON GIN PALACES

By the late 1820s England had long bid goodbye to the idea of prohibition, and London's increasing population established it as the largest city in the world. Distilling was becoming more refined and a newfound attention was placed on producing quality spirits. Illicit distilling existed, but was insignificant in comparison to the preceding century. Londoners with disposable income had a new, shinier alternative to drinking in dingy dark rooms. The birth of the London "gin palace" brought about new venues offering comfortable social atmospheres for patrons of the drink. In many ways it was London's contribution to the origin of the modern bar. Most were located in well-to-do neighborhoods and many people would stop in for a drink before a theatre show or on their way home from work.

A London gin palace, 1850.

Tom and Jerry Taking Blue Ruin After the Spell is Broke Up by I. R. and G. Cruikshank (1820).

One characteristic of an early gin palace was the utilization of the recently available gaslight to showcase their establishment. Owners invested in luxuriant moldings and large glass windows on the exteriors to attract customers. The interiors were not as detail-oriented, typically consisting of one long bar for patrons to stand by. Some did have wallpaper and decorative mirrors on the interiors to add ambiance.

A "flash of lightning," or a helping of gin, was not the only offering the palaces made available. Beer, rum, brandy and other libations were commonly sold as well, although gin remained paramount. As time passed, patrons wanted more out of their drinking establishment and their libations. Bigger palaces opened with room for dancing and more refined cocktail menus.

None of London's original gin palaces survive today, but there are many modern London venues, such as Graphic Bar located in London's Golden Square, whose décor and architecture are inspired by the original palaces.

GIN PALACE

95 AVENUE A
NEW YORK CITY, NEW YORK
WWW.GINPALACENY.COM

My wife, Katie, and I enter through a discrete entrance—a door we wandered past twice before discovering—into a dimly lit room featuring rich wooden stadium seating with buttoned leather cushioning across from a long copper bar lined with more bottles of gin than I have ever seen. Beautiful moldings and a decorative ceiling make a patron forget they're in the bustling Big Apple. I start drumming my palms to the music, British rock, as we walk up to the bar and are greeted by beverage director Frank Cisneros. He smiles and offers to show me around before I sit down at the bar to peruse his incredible gin selection. As he walks around the bar to welcome us, I notice what looks like a large horizontal freezer. "It's a block-ice maker," he says after observing my stare. "What benefits do you find in making your own ice?" I ask. "One of the big benefits is not having to rely on someone else to make and deliver blocks for you, not to mention the often hefty expense. We also have far more control over the type and size of blocks we make and can be

> "We thought a lot in the beginning about whether we wanted to be superlative in terms of carrying *every* gin, or be a bit more tailored and carry only what we consider to be the best. We've gone the latter route."

more efficient in making them, such as larger-sized blocks for punch, or two-inch by two-inch blocks for individual cocktails," Frank says.

We head downstairs to what appears to be a typical Manhattan service-industry basement. But it is not ordinary at all. There is a freezer that houses kegs, but not kegs filled with beer, tonic water, or club soda. These kegs are filled with premixed homemade gin and tonics. In later travels I would find a few more venues serving G&Ts on tap, such as Mockingbird Hill in Washington, DC, but this is my first and I am awestruck. Frank's enthusiasm for the process is contagious. We discuss the complications of bringing the cocktail to the tap both logistically and legally. Every state has individual laws pertaining to what you can and cannot do with alcohol. In terms of legal obstacles, Frank tells me about a New York law stating that any pressurized carbonated alcoholic drink must be in constant motion. His solution: place the kegs on magnetic stirring plates, like the ones you'd find in a chemistry lab. Voila! Legal G&Ts on tap in New York City.

"So how does this system work?" I ask. Frank answers, "We use five-gallon Cornelius kegs which are traditionally used in home-brew applications. There is a removable hatch, which allows us to fill and refill the kegs, seal them, and pressurize them using commercially available CO_2 tanks. They then fit onto a traditional bar's tap system via a converted hose. We use a slightly modified recipe, initially championed by our good

Police and Thieves

2 oz. London dry gin
½ oz. lime juice
½ oz. pineapple juice
¼ oz. grapefruit juice
½ oz. cinnamon syrup*
2 dashes Angostura bitters

Combine all ingredients in a cocktail shaker. Fill completely with ice and shake vigorously for 15 seconds. Strain into a cocktail coupe, being careful to strain out any ice chips or errant citrus pulp. Garnish with two striped dashes of Angostura, if desired. (*Cinnamon syrup: Break up one 8 oz. container's worth of cinnamon sticks and add them to 4 quarts of hot water. Heat to a boil, then reduce heat, cover and simmer for 45 minutes. Combine the resulting cinnamon water 1-to-1 with superfine sugar, by volume.)

friend Mayur Subbaro using London dry gin, Bittermens Commonwealth Tonic [a dry and bitter alcoholic tonic] and a bit of hopped grapefruit bitters. This results in a very dry and refreshingly bitter tonic that has been well received by our customers; it's darker and less filtered than your traditional gin and tonic and has a nice depth of flavor."

We head back upstairs and Frank mentions that the Gin Palace's premixed carbonated cocktails are not only for the tap. He explains, "A fellow up in Massachusetts named Matt Shellenberger developed a manifold that fits atop a traditional champagne bottle. What's special about his contraption is that when paired with a high-pressure regulator on a regular CO_2 tank, you can achieve really high levels of carbonation. The traditionally available carbonation systems for bottles aren't sufficient to get the sort of bubbles you would like in a gin and tonic. His system has allowed us to create mini gin and tonic pairings in single-serving bottles, meaning I create a flavored tonic, such as a eucalyptus and Egyptian mint tonic, and pair it with a local floral aromatic gin. I then carbonate that concoction and bottle it in small 187ml single-serving bottles. The result is a highly personalized gin and tonic with very pleasing botanical elements and nice refreshing bubbles."

As I sit down at the bar and Frank walks behind it, I slowly look through the gins lined up. I can already deduct that I am both in way over my head and in great company

Uzi Tenenbaum

1 ½ oz. London dry gin
½ oz. ginger syrup*
½ oz. Zucca (an Italian amaro)
¾ oz. lemon juice
Candied-ginger garnish
Top with soda

Combine all ingredients except soda in a cocktail shaker. Fill completely with ice and shake vigorously for 15 seconds. Strain into a Collins glass filled with ice. Top with soda and garnish with a piece of candied ginger. (*Ginger syrup: Rough peel 1 lb. ginger, cut into smaller pieces and extract juice using a hard juice extractor. Combine resulting ginger juice with 2 parts superfine sugar to 1 part ginger juice by volume at room temperature. Whisk vigorously to thoroughly dissolve sugar.)

MI5

¾ oz. Plymouth
¾ oz. Applejack (100 proof
American apple brandy)
¾ oz. Dolin sweet vermouth
¾ oz. Cynar (Italian amaro)

Combine all ingredients in a glass
stirring vessel, fill to the brim
with high quality ice, then crack
3 cubes of ice with the end of a
spoon and pack in. Stir vigorously
for 30 seconds. Strain into
a cocktail coupe.

to learn about gin. It's early in my research, but still, so many labels I had not seen before. I order a G&T on tap, of course, and its flavor is so much more sophisticated than the generic knockoffs I had imbibed in the past. Its color is a murky light brown, a footprint left from the tonic's natural cinchona bark. As I enjoy my cocktail, Frank and bartender Ryan Dolliver break out a couple new bottles of gin that they are considering adding to the bar. Ryan makes two identical cocktails, one with a new gin and a second with Beefeater, which they find to be a great classic-yet-neutral gin that is a good base for comparison. Frank blindly samples both cocktails and gives his review and verdict. They go through this process with a few gins, not all of which beat Beefeater. As I look over the menu I notice that, in fitting with the music overhead, all the house cocktails are named after British songs. Names such as "Irish Blood, English Heart" (Morrissey) and "Power, Corruption & Lies" (New Order) fill the page.

Looking at the menu and the bar, I note that although the gin selection is tremendous, a few popular mainstream brands are absent. Frank tells me, "There are many gins available today, which is refreshing, but as with anything some of them just aren't that great. We thought a lot in the beginning about whether we wanted to be superlative in terms of carrying every gin, or be a bit more tailored and carry only what we consider to be the best. We've gone the latter route and still managed to amass over seventy fantastic gins on offer for our guests." As one of my first stops on this adventure, I am eternally grateful for the hospitality they showed Katie and myself and the time they took to discuss their love of gin.

The "Holy War" crusade for temperance and prohibition
was often led by women and clergy in the nineteenth century.

United States Prohibition

By taking a close look at Prohibition, the viewer gazes not only on a transitory legal and social "experiment," but on a period in American history when people wanted change, power was shifting hands, and underground markets were born. The 18th Amendment was passed in America in 1920, outlawing all intoxicating alcohol, only to be repealed in 1933 by the 21st Amendment. Although alcohol was illegal in the 1920s, the nation remained thirsty and a massive underground demand surged through the US for a drink, just as it had in London two centuries prior. As it turned out, the law didn't stop most from seeking a sip, and secretive speakeasies and homemade producers ran rampant. Even politicians who voted for the 18th Amendment were known to continue their drinking practices. As actor Will Rogers remarked at the time, "Prohibition is better than no liquor at all."

The Ascent to Prohibition

Prohibition was not an idea born overnight. To understand the movement one must begin in the nineteenth century. By as early as the 1830s, the temperance movement's voice began to rise and spread the shadow of its wings across the country. An opening call for moderation, with offerings of a communal support network, resulting in an eventual ban on all alcohol, was the ambition. As its roots spread from Protestant churches, support, amongst women and men alike, was amassing energy and organization.

By the middle 1800s, with the endorsement from the all-male Liberty Party, the Women's Christian Temperance Union was gaining traction toward an alcohol-free America. Sin, as they saw it, was the great hindrance holding the nation back. After years of tolerating the saloon society that had become so popular amongst men, women wanted—and deserved—a change.

As the Civil War ended in 1865, immigrants from European countries such as Ireland, Italy, and Germany flooded to the streets of a burgeoning United States, bringing with them cultural traditions, diverse appetites and customs. Drink was everywhere, and many women and children found their lives in ruin by neglectful, abusive, or deceased husbands. From 1873 to 1874 the Woman's Crusade gained momentum in its pursuit of a dehydrated America. Women, holding little official political power at the time, used other strategies to spread their message of temperance such as demonstrations, petitions, and vigils. It was working. As Susan B. Anthony,

who was a member of the Temperance Union, stated, "Resolved, that the women of this nation in 1876, have greater cause for discontent, rebellion and revolution than the men of 1776."

Led by Frances Willard, the Women's Christian Temperance Union's message was becoming louder and stronger. In addition to a ban on alcohol, they sought to eliminate gambling, establish rights for children working in factories, convalesce the public education system, advance women's rights, and improve neglected slums. Although progressing, Prohibition would need a more focused voice if it were to succeed.

In 1893 a new organization formed in Ohio. The Anti-Saloon League, founded by Howard Hyde Russell, had only one goal—the ban of all alcohol. Where the number of objectives diluted the Temperance Union's message, the League's message was singular and clear-cut. The League's most notorious leader, Wayne Wheeler, was extremely successful in his lobbying efforts and strategy to partner with everyone who shared that one goal. Support was found throughout the country. From Democrats to Republicans, suffragists to the Ku Klux Klan, John D. Rockefeller to Andrew Carnegie, support was flowering. But America was still dependent on the revenue collected from the liquor tax, and until that changed, nothing else would.

In 1913 the United States passed an income tax amendment that provided the federal government a new revenue stream and alleviated the dependence on liquor taxes. The Anti-Saloon League moved quickly into action. With America's entry into the First World War, the sizeable German immigrant population—whose breweries and beer were cultural staples they brought with them—found themselves the target of the League's propaganda campaign. The campaign successfully linked alcohol with German-Americans and motivated public fear of an allegiance to the Fatherland. This was highly effective, and for the Prohibitionists the finish line was in sight. Both houses of Congress passed the 18th amendment in 1917 and the law went into effect in 1920. America was finally parched, but, as history patently retells us, you cannot stop an able-minded soul from attaining that which he or she desires.

THE ALMIGHTY LOOPHOLES

While illegal production of alcohol met the main demand for spirits during Prohibition, there were three loopholes that citizens used to their advantage:

1. Medicinal Alcohol: Distilleries were allowed to continue to produce spirits for medicinal use.

2. Fermenting Farmers: Farmers were allowed to pick and store fruit, in particular apples, for the purpose of fermenting. Apple juice became hard cider.

3. Religious Right: Catholic, Jewish, and other religious communities were allowed a stipend of sacramental wine for use in their services. In turn, services saw a massive spike in attendance within the first year of Prohibition. The United States also saw a rise in people claiming to be rabbis.

BATHTUB GIN

The term "bathtub gin" comes from the Prohibition era in the United States. Bathtub faucets were used to fill bottles and jugs too large to fit under a kitchen sink while diluting the mixture. Rumors also claim that bathtubs were actually used to mix the concoctions, a blend of subpar denatured grain alcohol and flavoring. In most locales quality distilled grain alcohol was not available because it was illegal and producers were forced to use less than reliable sources. Many ingredients could be found in bathtub gin, including juniper berry juice and glycerin. Standards of quality became so low in Prohibition America that people actually died from drinking poisonous juice. Today "bathtub gin" may be used to refer to any illegally made gin.

Researching and speaking with experts about alcohol prohibition in past centuries has led me to one belief: prohibition does not work. Gin's face has been scratched and scarred by the long nails of self-proclaimed "moral" outreach and "we-know-what-is-good-for-you" ideals. Still, gin stands tall whether in the shadows or the limelight. It is difficult to relate to these prohibitions of the past because we live in a society where alcohol is not only legal but ubiquitous. And yet around the globe we are still letting the powers that be dictate what we may or may not consume.

Providentially, the *spirit* of gin shows her face in all forms of rebellion.

As US Prohibition neared its demise, states slowly realized that there was tax revenue to be made by controlling the sale of spirits. The same is true in today's society, albeit with a slightly different recreational pursuit. The famous black markets of yesterday and today have never done anyone any good. And yet proponents of substance prohibition argue—in past and present—that morals would rise, jails would empty, and the populous would be better off without these substances. But what happened when they got their way? The exact opposite.

I was grateful to sit down with N.a. Poe—someone who is not afraid to speak out on modern US prohibition—to discuss how gin's notorious history relates to today's world.

I begin, "Why did Prohibition ultimately fail?"

Poe answers, "Prohibition doesn't work. Never has, never will. Vice is as American as apple pie."

"What are some of the negative effects you see stemming from the prohibitive legislation of the past? How do they translate to today?"

"We can learn a lot by examining US Prohibition in the early twentieth century, which created some of the most colorful gangsters our country has ever seen. Guys like Al Capone, Arnold Rothstein, and Lucky Luciano have been romanticized for decades in cinema and print. But these guys used violence and corruption to rule their day. And it all started with gin—or more accurately, Prohibition. Gin was the illegal resource they used to make money and terrorize the public, just like marijuana and marijuana dealers today. It didn't work then and doesn't work now."

"What are some of the other by-products of Prohibition that current voters should be studying as they choose their stance today?"

"Destroying families, overcrowding prisons, and clogging courtrooms with victimless trials has done nothing to stop the use of marijuana, just as Prohibition did nothing to curtail gin consumption. Supporters of Prohibition guaranteed that the prisons would be emptied once alcohol was removed from society, but because of the black market that arose, the opposite was true—Prohibition filled the prisons to capacity."

"Comparing the legalization of alcohol with today's evolving landscape, what role did the voice of the people play?"

"Public sentiment about the 18th Amendment began to turn when it became clear that it was not delivering its intended result, and was in fact aggravating the social problems—drunkenness, crime, mental illness, and poverty—that Prohibition promised to eliminate. The rallying cries to end Prohibition were heard across America, and that growing chorus finally led to the end of Prohibition via the 21st Amendment."

Poe leaves me quoting American journalist H. L. Mencken, who wrote this in 1925: "Five years of Prohibition have had, at least, this one benign effect: they have completely disposed of all the favorite arguments of the prohibitionists. None of the great boons and usufructs that were to follow the passage of the 18th Amendment has come to pass. There is not less drunkenness in the Republic, but more. There is not less crime, but more. There is not less insanity, but more. The cost of government is not smaller, but vastly greater. Respect for law has not increased, but diminished."

I thank Poe for his time and realize that we are still fighting yesterday's battles today. But I feel comfort in the knowledge that the rebellious spirit of gin shall always prevail.

N.a. Poe is a comedian and activist, founder of The Panic Hour, *and creator of a monthly civil disobedience action,* Smoke Down Prohibition, *that is approaching its one-year anniversary. His work has been recognized and featured in* Vice *and* High Times *magazines, where he was honored as the September 2013 Freedom Fighter of the Month.*

FAMOUS GIN

Gin has seen its fair share of both praise and censure. The juniper-based spirit has appealed, throughout history, to many in the limelight—writers and actors, musicians and politicians, producers and painters. Although the arts have been used many times to defame gin, as exemplified in Hogarth's *Gin Lane* print, it is also useful to take a peek at how celebrity, numerous times, has brought gin into popular fashion.

Besides the stories below, many other figureheads, including Humphrey Bogart, Frank Sinatra, Tennessee Williams, and Dean Martin, advanced gin's image and enticed their audiences to partake. Mae West, Dorothy Parker, and Jack London are all names linked to the martini. Politicians such as Winston Churchill, who preferred no vermouth in his glass of gin, and Franklin Delano Roosevelt both promoted the martini. Even modern television shows aimed at a young market have used the martini as a prop representing societal social structure. Homer Simpson exemplifies this when he states, "He knows just how I like my martini—full of alcohol."

> "I would like to observe the vermouth from across the room while I drink my martini."
> —Winston Churchill

BESSIE SMITH (1894–1937)

American blues singer Bessie Smith had the voice of an angel and she performed with all her soul. She began as a dancer in minstrel shows and cabarets, but soon made the transition to singing and eventually to having her own touring show. In 1920 she signed a record contract with Columbia Records and began a successful career that produced over 150 recordings.

Included in her catalog are two songs she released under the title "Gin House Blues." The first, a tale of a heartbroken woman who goes to the gin house to drink away her sorrow, was recorded in 1926. The second recording, initially titled "Me and My Gin," was released in 1928 and is the more widely known version today. Neither song praises gin, but they

"Of all the gin joints in all the towns in all the world, she walks into mine."
—Humphrey Bogart, *Casablanca*

do reflect gin's importance during this period. Keep in mind these songs were released during Prohibition and demonstrate the openness with which speakeasies were discussed.

As a beautiful, profitable, business-savvy black woman who wasn't afraid to travel and perform in a time when segregation was predominant, she became a figurehead for both women's rights and racial equality. Unfortunately she died at the young age of 43 in a car accident in Mississippi.

Her voice lives on as other musicians draw inspiration from her. Nina Simone covered "Gin House Blues" on her 1961 album *Forbidden Fruit*, bringing Smith's vitality back to modern ears. Janis Joplin, who herself was known to tipple a bit, drew inspiration from Smith's soul-soaked voice as she crafted her own musical tone; in fact, she was such a big fan that she bought a proper headstone for Smith's grave.

> Frank Sinatra: "Let me fix you a martini that's pure magic."
> Dean Martin: "It may not make life's problems disappear, but it'll certainly reduce their size."

EXCERPT FROM "GIN HOUSE BLUES"

By Harry Burke (possibly a pseudonym for James C. Johnson)

Stay away from me
Cause I'm in my sin
Stay away from me
Cause I'm in my sin
If this joint is raided
Somebody get me my gin
Don't try me nobody
Cause you will never win

> "Happiness is . . . finding two olives in your martini when you're hungry."
> —Johnny Carson

ERNEST HEMINGWAY, 1899–1961

Hemingway's novels held cocktails in high regard and spirits were often utilized in his detailed imagery. He is even credited with inventing a few unique cocktails throughout his writings, adventures and collaborations abroad.

During time spent in Venice, Italy, in the mid-twentieth century, Hemingway frequented a group of select establishments including Harry's Bar. He mentions Harry's Bar several times in his novel *Across the River and into the Trees* (1950). He was a regular and would be welcomed through the door to his reserved table. (Turn to the feature on page 124 for a detailed account of Harry's Bar and the martini they are famous for.)

As well as the martini at Harry's, Hemingway wrote about other gin-based cocktails including the gin and tonic, the white lady, and the Tom Collins. The white lady was a favorite while in Paris with fellow author F. Scott Fitzgerald. The gimlet, constructed from two ounces gin and one-and-a-half ounces fresh-squeezed lime juice, is also featured in Hemingway's *The Short Happy Life of Francis Macomber* (1936).

The Green Isaacs special, a creation that Hemingway is credited with originating in his novel *Islands in the Stream* (1970), is titled after the Isaacs Islands. This manuscript was discovered with many other writings after Hemingway's death and published posthumously.

Green Isaacs Special

1½ oz. gin
2 oz. green coconut water
½ oz. fresh lime juice
2 drops Angostura bitters

Combine ingredients in a shaker and either stir or shake. Strain into a rocks glass.

EXCERPT FROM ISLANDS IN THE STREAM BY ERNEST HEMINGWAY

"Where Thomas Hudson lay on the mattress his head was in the shade cast by the platform at the forward end of the flying bridge where the controls were and when Eddy came aft with the tall cold drink made of gin, lime juice, green coconut water, and chipped ice with just enough Angostura bitters to give it a rusty, rose color, he held the drink in the shadow so the ice would not melt while he looked out over the sea."

"I like to have a martini,
two at the very most;
three, I'm under the table,
four I'm under my host!"
—Dorothy Parker

BOND, JAMES BOND

Today, many immediately think of James Bond when they hear the word martini. Bond first orders a martini in Ian Fleming's 1953 novel *Casino Royale*, instructing the barman to make him a dry martini in detail, saying, "Three measures of Gordon's, one of vodka, half a measure of Kina Lillet. Shake it very well until it's ice-cold, then add a large thin slice of lemon peel." A "vesper martini," as it later became known, contains both gin and vodka, although gin is the prominent ingredient. Let it be known that Mr. Bond actually ordered more vodka martinis, as well as other cocktails, than gin martinis throughout his escapades, but we won't hold that against him. He epitomized the sophisticated cocktail experience and is still the face many see reflecting on the surface of their placid crisp martini.

A key component to the vesper, Kina Lillet (a French aperitif wine) may be found today labeled as Lillet Blanc. The name change correspondingly reflects a recipe adjustment. Lillet has been modified to stay with the times, offering a less bitter taste. Due to this, many suggest adding a dash of bitters to supplement when making a vesper.

The cocktail has been judged poorly by some, but with the increase in unique gin labels being produced, enjoying a vesper with a subtler gin that allows the Lillet's flavor to have impact can generate an upstanding cocktail.

Vesper Martini

3 oz. Gordon's gin
1 oz. vodka
½ oz. Kina Lillet (Lillet Blanc)
Lemon peel garnish
Optional dash of bitters

Combine all ingredients into a shaker and shake, strain into a martini glass, and add garnish.

BEEFEATER

A little more to pay – a lot more to enjoy

This is the luxury gin — triple distilled from grain for extra dryness. Gin, that is clear as a diamond, soft as velvet. True, Beefeater costs a little more than ordinary gin, but what a difference. Have some today.

37/-
a bottle

EXTRA DRY
BEEFEATER GIN

JAMES BURROUGH LIMITED, LONDON, S.E.11. DISTILLERS OF FINE GIN SINCE 1820

Beefeater ad from 1960.

DUKES BAR

DUKES HOTEL
ST. JAMES'S PLACE, LONDON, ENGLAND
WWW.DUKESHOTEL.COM

Nestled within Dukes Hotel in the St. James section of London sits Dukes Bar, one of the classiest yet most tranquil venues I've visited. After being seated and kindly asked to remove my hat, Alessandro Palazzi, Dukes' resident cocktail specialist, wheels his cocktail trolley toward our table. We order martinis, each to be made with a different one of his favorite gins. Palazzi is happy to make recommendations, and returns shortly with bottles and glasses right from the freezer. Not a cube of ice in sight.

He informs us that this is his own vermouth, made by him and his friends, as he pours a small amount into the glass, swirls it around, and proceeds to dump the liquid on the floor—carpeted, no less! This is sometimes called an "in & out martini," due to the fact that the vermouth is only used to coat the glass and then discarded. This martini depends on a quality gin and extremely aromatic lemon. He peels a twist of lemon,

Alessandro Palazzi

"The first thing I learned, being a bartender, is that you learn every day."

The Vesper
Martini
(Dukes style)

2.4 oz. (70ml) of No.3 Gin
.8 oz. (25ml) of Potoki vodka
.2 oz. (5ml) of Dukes amber
vermouth
3 drops of Angostura bitters
Fresh organic orange zest

Place 3 dashes of bitters in
a frozen martini glass and swirl.
Add vermouth, then vodka, then
gin. Squeeze the organic orange
zest over the glass so that a drop of
oil falls into the cocktail. Garnish
with same orange zest. (Note: the
glass and spirits come straight
from the freezer.)

squeezes a drop into the glass, and fills it with gin. My Warner Edwards martini is crisp and refreshing and has some intriguing botanicals, perhaps cardamom, out in front.

I ask Alessandro to describe his vermouth, in particular as it compares and contrasts with American vermouths.

"The difference in the vermouth I make with Sacred Distillery [in London] is that all the ingredients we use come from UK, as well as the wine. The alcohol content is thirty-six proof. In the US, they infuse different kinds of spices, but I've noticed that many bartenders are now trying to copy my style of vermouth. My vermouth is also not on the market, except in Japan. I think the vermouth is getting an exposure like bitters a few years ago, and I think this is very healthy for the cocktail industry."

I was very entertained by Alessandro pouring the vermouth onto the floor after coating the glass, and had to ask him about it.

"This is part of the theatre. When I took over the bar, the previous bartender used to do a 'move' while twisting the lemon, and at the beginning people were surprised I wasn't doing it as well, asking at the same time why we didn't shake the martini. So I came out with this gimmick of shaking the vermouth on the floor just to give the making of the martini a bit of theatrical flavor."

"It works!" I say, and continue, "The dialog between customer and mixologist seems to be of great importance at Dukes. How does the mobile cocktail cart add to customers' overall experience while drinking at Dukes?" Alessandro replies, "Dukes was the first one to serve the martini from the trolley, and that gives an overall experience to the customer where we show the customers how we make the Dukes martini. And it also allows me to show people the products I use, especially because I work with many small gin distilleries that share the same passion as me."

"You mentioned that the lemons you used to garnish our martinis were of special importance. Where are they from, and what qualities do they have that contribute to the perfect martini?" I ask. He replies, "The organic lemons come from Amalfi [Italy], and the reason why I use them is because when you freeze gin or vodka, the spirit becomes thicker. So when I squeeze the oil out of the skin of the lemons, it will float on top of the martini glass and when you pick the glass up to drink your martini, the first thing you will notice is the smell of the lemons coming out of it." (It would not be until I was sitting across the globe with Derek Brown sipping his martini at the Columbia Room in Washington, DC—see page 130—that I would fully appreciate how gin texturally develops when stored in the freezer. I knew it was something good in London, but upon a second glance I am hooked.)

After he mentions his future travel plans to the US and Japan, I ask Alessandro to describe how other parts of the world have influenced his cocktails. "The first thing I learned, being a bartender, is that you learn every day," he tells me. "I am very lucky as over the last two years, I had the chance to travel in different parts of the world and meet several different styles of bartenders. But in common we have the same passion of making drinks, and this is an excellent learning experience, even for an old bartender like me!"

Meeting Alessandro toward the beginning of my journey into the world of gin was a true blessing. Just watching him make a cocktail motivated me to seek that same passion in each destination I visited. Gin is an art, and those who create it and mix it are using their intellect to balance flavors and stimulate taste buds.

Classic Dukes Martini

.2 oz. (5ml) of Dukes dry vermouth
3.2 oz. (95ml) of Sacred gin
Fresh organic lemon zest

Pour vermouth in a frozen martini glass and swirl. Add the gin. Twist the lemon zest over the glass so that a drop of oil falls into the cocktail. Garnish with the same twist of organic lemon from Amalfi. (Note: the glass and gin come straight from the freezer.)

THE
ART & CRAFT
of DISTILLATION

hen most consumers order a gin cocktail or purchase a bottle of gin at the spirit shop, they are unaware of the many variables distillers have to select from when fashioning their libation. And the recent gin revival has only complicated matters, much to the delight of the consumer.

Today's producers make choices regarding the distillation method, the number of distillation rounds, the flavor profile (the combination of herbs, spices, fruit and other botanicals), and the storage system used before bringing their product to market. As time, technology, and the regional interests of bartenders and drinkers have evolved, so too have the distillation methods by which gin is made.

In short, to distill is to separate a liquid into its component parts by heating the liquid into vapor form. Since alcohol (172° F) boils at a lower temperature than water (212° F), by using controlled heating methods one can purify the distillate from low-alcohol fermented liquid into a cocktail-worthy spirit.

The three main distillation methods are: pot-distilled, cold-compound, and column-distilled. But variations abound. Hendrick's Distillery in Scotland currently uses a combination of the Bennett still (aka pot still) and the Carter-head still (a pot feeding a column). The Botanist gin, also produced in Scotland, is made using a rare Lomond still, which is a cross between a pot and a column still.

The choice of botanicals used during the distillation process has also increased greatly from traditional methods, with a wide variety available locally and from around the globe. Monkey 47, a German-produced gin, uses an astounding 47 botanicals to create their unique flavor profile. Makers of the Botanist send gatherers out to find the exact botanical specimens they desire in their native Scotland. And once the botanicals are in hand, makers have to choose how to infuse them. During the distillation process, some makers choose to directly steep the botanicals in the base spirit to impart aromatics, while others enclose them in cotton sacks and either place them directly in the base-spirit still-basin or hang the sacks above, allowing the vapors to pass through them as they rise. After production is complete, many distillers have taken to producing a second gin label that is aged in gin barrels. In the Caribbean old rum casks have been used, bourbon casks in the US, while others use fresh oak

The impressive copper pot still at Corsair Distillery, Nashville, Tennessee.

barrels. This results in an aged aromatic quality imparting some of the subtleties of a whiskey.

As we move through the early twenty-first century, distillers are limited only by their imaginations when choosing the methods and components in crafting their gin. As chemistry advances and the human imagination swells with wonder, we can gratefully expect to see some new additions and practices to the world of distillation in the coming years.

GIN BLENDING

Gin blending does not seem to be a common practice currently and is not mentioned in historical records, but I do believe it will come into fashion as it has with whiskey. At least, it should. Sacred Distillery in London produces a kit of individual gins, each distilled with a sole botanical meant to be blended with another by the consumer to taste. Modern gins behave very differently on individual palates, and I have found, just like food, what is delicious to some sends others back in recoil. As blending different whiskey batches and labels is in such popular fashion today, both cocktail craftsmen and adventurous home tipplers should strive to break the commonly accepted limitations of gin and create a new horizon based on the premise that anything is possible—because with gin, it is. Combining a soft subtle gin with another more aggressive one in proper ratio can produce a new flavor profile entirely. The gins of today have such diverse qualities and such widespread reach that someday, perhaps, gins from every continent may be gathered and blended into the "Gin of the Earth." And what an Earth that would be.

Heads, Hearts, and Tails

The distilling process is made up of several timely events. *Heads, hearts* and *tails* are terms used by distillers to indicate the three byproducts of a distillation run. But before the heads make an appearance, the first elements of the distillate to vaporize and rise are referred to as foreshots. These vapors contain unwanted congeners that are produced during fermentation, such as methanol and acetone and other less palatable substances. These vapors are extracted from the still and discarded.

Heads refer to the cap on top of a still that captures the rising vapor, which is then pulled through a tube, termed an *arm*, to be collected

and cooled back into a more potent and purer form of spirit. Depending on the still's temperature and the botanicals being harnessed, these collected vapors may be kept or discarded. Modern gin producers sometimes include the heads in the final product in an effort to capture something new and unique.

Hearts consist of the core distillate that provides the desired high-level alcohol, along with the desirable congeners.

Tails are the last to go, and we don't want them. Typically the final vapors that collect and turn back into liquid have nothing to offer in either substantial alcohol content or taste enhancement, so these are usually cast off.

Distillers at Corsair tend to their traditional pot still.

Pot-Distilled Gin

This is where gin began. The process historically consists of two rounds of distillation. Customarily it begins using a copper pot to distill fermented mash from grains, typically barley, wheat, rye or maize. Molasses is also employed as a source for the neutral base spirit. After the first round of distillation, juniper berries and other botanicals are added to the distillate, which is refined a second time to impart the desired flavor profile. Pot stills remain a popular choice today and are used by distilleries as diverse as Philadelphia Distilling (Bluecoat), Corsair Distillery (Corsair) and Black Friars Distillery (Plymouth). Broker's—crafted in a 200-year-old distillery in Birmingham, England—has this to say on their website: "The distillery uses only traditional pot stills. Continuous distillation using column stills is more efficient and is used by the major brands, but pot stills are better for extracting maximum flavour from the botanicals in a traditional hand-crafted fashion."

Not all distilleries make their own base spirit. Some distillers procure it from a third party, adding to it the desired flavor-profile to create their gin. Some are passionate about creating something from the ground up, whereas others are in tune with the beneficial collaborative effort that a community brings to the bottle. Both produce some incredible and diverse results.

COLD-COMPOUND GIN

Cold-compound distilling is considered a less desirable production method, generally used by many large distillers to create sizeable quantities of product. This type of gin is made by adding juniper and other natural botanicals and flavorings to the neutral base spirit without additional distillation. It is an infusion without any purification. There are, however, independent distillers today that are utilizing this method to create distinctive spirits. By utilizing this method without the goal of mass production, great time and care can be put into this style of production. Master of Malt's Bathtub Gin, produced by Professor Cornelius Ampleforth, offers six extremely small-batch varieties using the cold-compound technique. Some runs only produce 30 to 60 bottles. Luckily there are small samples available for purchase on the Internet.

COLUMN-DISTILLED GIN

The design of the column still has undergone many revisions as distilling practices have evolved, but it didn't come into widespread popularity until the invention of the Coffey still, patented in 1830 by Irishman Aeneas Coffey. Coffey improved upon still designs by predecessors Sir Anthony Perrier and Robert Stein. By adding two pipes to Stein's design, Coffey was able to create a system where a greater percentage of alcohol vapors recirculated into the still, producing

Corsair Negroni

1½ oz. Corsair barrel-aged gin
1½ oz. sweet vermouth
1½ oz. Campari
Orange-twist garnish

Mix ingredients in an old-fashioned glass over ice. Stir and drop in garnish. May also be prepared and served neat in a chilled cocktail glass.

Pegu Club

2 oz. Professor Cornelius Ampleforth's Bathtub Gin Navy-Strength
¾ oz. Cointreau
½ oz. fresh lime juice
1 dash Angostura bitters
1 dash orange bitters

Place all ingredients in a shaker over ice. Shake (or stir) and strain into a chilled cocktail glass.

CORSAIR
GIN
44% ALC/VOL (88 PROOF)

GIN-HEAD STYLE AMERICAN GIN

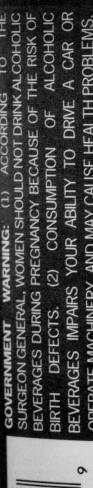

8 99119 00204 9

Citrusy, Smooth, Unique. Crafted for Cocktails.

We make our gin in very small batches using the gin-head basket on our hand-hammered pot still. This uncommon step brings out bright flavors and mutes sharp notes, making for a smooth and approachable gin. We're proud to use an unusual mix of traditional botanicals to give our gin a clearly unique and satisfying character.

100% grain neutral spirits

We welcome your feedback – come visit us online and let us know your thoughts! And grab recipes, or share yours, while you're at our site.

http://www.corsairartisan.com

a lighter-tasting higher-proof gin with less impurities. This also negated the need for multiple distillations and therefore saved time.

Each column (stills may have anywhere from a single to several columns) is basically comprised of a series of small pot stills, and as the vapors rise through the column's chambers, they become purer. That is not to say that modern distillers using this method only distill once. Many use multiple distillation rounds to impart different botanicals' flavors to the base. For example, botanicals such as elderflower do better when distilled at a lower temperature than other botanicals. A column still may also be referred to as a "continuous still," signifying that it can unceasingly produce spirits.

San Francisco's Distillery No. 209 produces their base spirit for No. 209 gin using four rounds of distillation in a column still. After the base spirit, made from Midwestern corn, is ready, they use a copper alembic pot to first macerate and then distill the final product with their botanical lineup, which includes juniper berries, cardamom pods, and angelica root. After the spirit is distilled, the correct ABV of 46% is reached by mixing it with snowmelt water from the Sierra-Nevada Mountains.

No. 209 Aviation

2 oz. No. 209 gin
¾ oz. fresh lemon juice
½ oz. maraschino liqueur
¼ oz. crème de violette

Combine the first three ingredients over ice in a shaker and shake until chilled. Strain into a chilled martini glass and drizzle the crème de violette over top. Garnish with a twist of lemon, if desired. Note: For a fully mixed Aviation, combine all ingredients before shaking.

GIN VARIETIES

GENEVER (OR JENEVER)

Although much different from the London and American dry gins that are widely consumed today, the original "gin" is credited to the Dutch, who in the late Middle Ages first used juniper berries and other botanicals to flavor malt wine, made from fermented wheat and barley malt, in a basic pot still. Producing this style of genever consisted of three rounds of distillation to create the malt wine, purifying and refining it with each round. Finally a fourth distillation would take place with the addition of all the botanicals resulting in an oude genever. Juniper in particular was chosen as a flavoring agent due to its supposed medicinal qualities and widespread availability, and the resulting spirit would often be stored in oak casks, aging the liquid and producing a heavier and generally sweeter spirit than we consider gin today.

Although different styles of gin evolved from the original over the centuries, genever continued to be made in its original form, or close to it. Then, during World War I, while malt supplies were scant, recipe

Illustration from the book The Newe [sic] Jewell of Health *by Conrad Gesner (1576).*

modifications had to be made. Lack of malt led to the popularity of a new style, jonge genever, which was produced using possible combinations of fermented sugarbeet, molasses and wheat, and was generally only distilled once, resulting in a less appealing sip.

There are several classifications of genever, or "Dutch Courage" as it is called, and distilleries are producing different varieties today.

Amsterdam Cocktail

2 oz. genever
1 oz. fresh orange juice
¾ oz. triple sec
3 dashes orange bitters

Pour all ingredients into a shaker over ice. Shake (or stir) and strain into a chilled cocktail glass.

GENEVER STYLES

1. Oude Genever (old style): Must contain at least 15% malt wine, and no more than 20 grams of sugar per liter.

2. Jonge Genever (young style): Must not contain more than 15% malt wine, and a maximum of 10 grams of sugar per liter.

3. Korenwijn (grain wine): Must contain between 51–70% malt wine, and no more than 20 grams of sugar per liter.

4. Auxiliary Variations: Other varieties of genever include bessen, fruit, hasselt, peket, balegem, citroen, corenwyn, and corn wine.

OLD TOM GIN

Old Tom is gin's middle child. It is the link between the juniper-based malty Dutch genever and the crisp London and American dry gin styles that are most popular today. Old Tom makes it easy to see the historical progression and evolution of gin's texture and flavor.

English makers during the end of the eighteenth century took original Dutch genever—with its full-bodied and most often sugary flavor—and adapted it to produce Old Tom, a lighter and less-sweet variation. It did however closely resemble genever. Beginning in 1830 with the patent of a continuous still by Aeneas Coffey, the improvements to the column still provided more palatable gins that didn't need sweetening and offered faster production, and as a result, Old Tom momentarily lost popularity in favor of the London dry style. It is a good thing for today's cocktail drinkers that many mixologists dutifully seek out historical rarities, and that a newfound demand for the Old Tom style has attracted the attention of some distilleries.

Two labels of note are Seestedt's Ransom Old Tom gin and Hayman's Old Tom gin. These are created using distinctive processes and produce two very different results, revealing that even within a specific style of gin the variations may be vast. Hayman's appears clear, while Ransom is a subtle brown, and the color variation between the two is definitely reflected in their taste.

Ransom's color is achieved by shortly aging the spirit in wine barrels that impart a drier and more tannin-filled sip.

Historic Ramos Gin Fizz

1½ oz. Old Tom gin
1 tbsp. simple syrup
½ oz. fresh lemon juice
½ oz. fresh lime juice
1 fresh egg white
1 oz. heavy cream
3 drops orange flower water
1 oz. club soda

Combine all ingredients except the club soda in a shaker without ice, and shake vigorously to froth the egg white for several minutes as the ingredients mix. Add ice to the shaker and shake again for several more minutes. Strain into a glass, top with club soda, and stir. (Note: Frothing the egg white before and after adding ice helps aerate the egg and produces a silky texture.)

The Gin-shop *by George Cruikshank, printed in Charles Dickens'* Sketches by Boz *(1836).*

Historically modeled, Ransom's recipe blends malted barley with high-proof corn-based spirit, which is then infused with botanicals. During the final distillation, Seestedt utilizes an alembic pot still that preserves the character of the spirit.

Hayman's adds sugar, a common practice historically, which results in a sweeter variation. Try mixing a Tom Collins or a Ramos fizz with an Old Tom gin. As bartenders acquire new Old Tom productions, modern takes on old recipes are not only reviving classic cocktails but also inspiring innovation. Old Tom appears to be making a comeback.

LONDON & NEW AMERICAN DRY GINS

By far the most popular style with the broadest range of variety, dry gin, also called London gin (if it's made in London, technically speaking), fills cocktail shakers around the globe nightly these days. In general, dry gin is not sweet. It is crisp and usually utilizes citrus fruits in the botanicals blend to give it a cool, sharp flavor. In London, dry gin is classified as agriculturally sourced ethyl alcohol, redistilled with botanicals including juniper berries, to produce a distillate that is a minimum of 70% alcohol by volume (ABV). Dyes and artificial flavorings are not allowed, and no more than 0.1 grams of sugar per liter is permitted. The final product must be at least 37.5% ABV. Most gins fall in the range of 40–47% ABV. The term "London dry gin" has ingrained its presence through longevity and is even used on some labels not produced in England. Let the debate ensue! The fact is, London gin has become synonymous with that particular style and preparation of the spirit, much the way brand eponyms like Xerox and Google are words used beyond their initial proprietary bounds.

Bluecoat's American Sling

1 ½ oz. Bluecoat American dry gin
¾ oz. fresh lemon juice
1 oz. pineapple juice
½ oz. simple syrup
2 dashes Angostura bitters

Combine all ingredients over ice in a tumbler and shake. Strain into an ice-filled highball glass or pint glass. Top with club soda. Garnish with lemon or lime peel.

New American dry gin is something relatively fresh and original—it's America's take on the London dry style. Definitely inspired by the London variety but without the same restrictions and with different ingredient sources, America has been giving the dry gin market a fresh vitality for the past decade. American gins are known to pull juniper back within the flavor profile, bringing it to a more even level with some of the other more aromatic botanicals. It should be noted that not all American gins are considered dry, and some are far more aromatic than a classic London dry. England is certainly seeing a surge in new productions as well, but British distillers have been schooled in the available local botanicals for centuries whereas US makers are in somewhat uncharted territory. Yet America has a wide range of climates and terrains that cultivate different and unique ingredients, providing a kid-in-a-candy-store opportunity for botanical-savvy distillers. Germany, Australia, Scotland, Japan, and even Russia (with its notorious vodka culture) produce a limited number of gins. America, however, has seen an astonishing number of new distilleries producing gin in the past decade.

As many US distilleries—such as Philadelphia Distilling, producers of Bluecoat American gin—researched their desired flavor profile, they looked to their home soil for inspiration. Bluecoat uses organic American citrus peels on their botanical canvas. Spokane, Washington's Dry Fly Distilling takes pride in

embracing "the farm to bottle approach," and they only use locally grown raw materials from sustainable farms.

American gins are quite diverse, and at the same time unique from other countries' gins, and US makers have infused a valuable component to the spirit of gin. Someday, not too long from now, "American gin" may be its own type of spirit, with its own classifications, regulations and personality. At the moment, we are witnessing the Wild West of American gin. One thing's for sure, dry-style gin isn't going away anytime soon, as it is spurred on by beautiful tradition and the spirit of invention.

Sloe Gin & Variants

Throughout history many fruit-flavored gins have come and gone, including various productions of orange and lemon gin. One that is making a comeback today is sloe gin, which uses sloe berries and other botanicals for flavor. The sloe berry is native to much of Europe, northwest Africa, and western Asia, and has been imported for growth in locales such as New Zealand. The sloe berry grows on the blackthorn tree, a thorny shrub that is often used in Britain for security hedges—nature's barbwire.

Greenhook Ginsmiths: The Dorstone

1 oz. Greenhook Beach Plum gin liqueur
1 oz. Greenhook American dry gin
½ oz. Dolin Blanc vermouth
½ oz. Bonal Gentiane-Quina
2 dashes Angostura bitters
Orange peel garnish

Combine gins, vermouth, Bonal, and bitters in a mixing glass.
Add ice and stir. Strain into a cocktail glass. Garnish with a burnt
orange peel (if you don't know how to flame a citrus peel,
many instructional videos are online).

Sloe gin, in general, maintains a juniper essence but balances it with the tart sweetness of a plum. *Sloes* are referred to as berries, but they are actually a member of the plum family. And as such, it is important to consider distilling temperature because of their fragile nature and tendency to undesirably transform under extreme heat.

Another British, and now American, variation is "damson gin," which is made from macerating damson plums in gin and sugar. New York-produced Averell Dansom Gin Liqueur is a relatively new American take on a damson gin.

Today, variations on sloe gin offer a great canvas for distillers to feature locally sourced ingredients native to their region and climate. Producers such as Monkey 47, Plymouth, Sipsmith, Hawker's, Chase, and Gordon's offer sloe gins in their lineup. Steven DeAngelo, of Greenhook Ginsmiths in Brooklyn, New York, produces a seasonal American Beach Plum Gin Liqueur that brings a fresh taste to an old classic. Beach plums are sloe berries' American cousin, and local growers enable Steven to procure fresh quality fruit for his juice.

Squires Dry Gin ad from 1966.

SLOE GIN FIZZ — Put two lumps of ice in a highball glass. Add a jigger of Old Mr. Boston Sloe Gin, the balance of ginger ale or sparkling water. Juice of one-half lemon if desired.

Old

Mr.Boston

SLOE GIN

DROP EVERYTHING AND TRY IT

A tingling, delicious glass of cool joy. A wine-like, thirst-quenching sloe gin fizz, sparkling with life and delightfully refreshing. Feel it soothe your parched palate. Not sweet—nor tart. But the interesting tangy flavor of Irish Sloe Berries, used for centuries to make a famous wine. Inviting. Tempting. Beautifully different in flavor. The secret of this glorious fizz is superb Old Mr. Boston—America's finest sloe gin. Made with genuine imported sloe berries, it should cost more, yet it costs about *half* as much as some other brands. Taste this great drink—it's incomparable.

Vintage ad from 1935.

THE "GIN IS ONLY GREAT FOR MIXING" CONSPIRACY

I have heard time and time again that the reason gin is a great spirit is because it is so good for mixing cocktails with, and historically that is correct. I do agree, but I must say—and maybe it was just my extreme exposure to gin over the course of researching and writing this book—I really like gin on the rocks. Taking 2 oz. of Germany-produced Monkey 47, stirring it quickly with a single ice cube to cool it down, and sipping it is quite an enjoyable experience for me and many friends who were convinced to partake. Today, with so many varieties and uniquely flavorful gins available, my taste buds have come to believe that gin has a lot to offer without the assistance of any other ingredients. I have heard the contrary spoken so many times from those who I respect most in the industry, but I must admit, I believe gin to be wonderful on its own. And I'm not the only one.

AUXILIARY GIN PHRASES

BARREL-AGED GIN

Although gin has not historically been aged for flavor, distilled gin may be stored in wooden casks to give it a heavy essence, that more closely resembles a whiskey or genever. Barrel-aged gins are becoming a popular variation for distilleries to produce, and they vary in color, nose, and flavor. Corsair, Waterloo, and Ransom all currently produce aged gins, with more coming to market regularly. These gins do have something new to bring to the bar when used in a negroni or a Martinez.

Some distillers, such as Corsair (Nashville, Tennessee), age gin in barrels.

DOUBLE GIN

Double gin, often created via the pot-distillation method, simply means that the producer includes a second round of distillation using more botanicals, which results in a higher-proof gin (76% ABV vs. 68% ABV).

GIN CORDIALS AND LIQUEURS

Cordials and liqueurs are synonymous terms used to describe a sweet liqueur, in this case with a gin base. Generally made with a combination of fruit, herbs, spices, sugars or sweetening syrup, cream, and other botanicals, cordials most often fall in the lighter-proof spectrum (30–70 proof). Sloe gins generally reside in this category, as well. At 36 proof, Raisthorpe Manor's Raspberry Gin Liqueur, from Yorkshire, offers a nectar that lends itself well to mixing with prosecco, cava, champagne, or any quality sparkling wine.

Navy Strength Gin

As its name suggests, navy strength gin is the robust parent in the gin family. Plymouth's navy strength label clocks in at a powerful 57% ABV (which is the defined minimum). In the early nineteenth century, gin was the liquor of choice among the British Royal Navy officers, and the drink accompanied sailors on many journeys. The initial demand for this ultra-potent potion rose out of practicality. Not everyone aboard the ship was awarded daily rations of gin. Gin had to be locked up and stored with the gunpowder and, on the rough seas, occasionally the spirit would spill or leak. If the gin was not at least 57% ABV, or 114 proof, the contaminated gunpowder would be ruined. In addition, they benefitted from having a higher-proof beverage taking up the same cargo footprint.

Some navy strength gins being produced today include bottles from New York Distilling Company (Perry Tot), Hayman's (Royal Dock of Deptford), and Leopold Brothers of Denver, Colorado. Try substituting a navy strength gin in your next Martinez.

One-Shot & Two-Shot Distillation Methods

The shot system describes an option distillers have when choosing how to distill their product. One-shot refers to using a botanical ratio that yields a spirit that only needs to be blended with water upon distillation to produce bottle-strength merchandise. The two-shot method saves time for some distilleries—especially the big, internationally distributed ones—by doubling the botanicals to neutral-spirit ratio, macerating them to release their juices, then distilling. Many distillers let the botanical blend macerate in the neutral spirit for up to 48 hours before beginning distillation. Once the distillation is complete, another portion of neutral alcohol, equal to the first, is blended along with water to dilute to bottling proof, resulting in twice as much product.

It may also be said that some distillers have taken to distilling each botanical separately and blending them after as a viable method, not a shortcut. Leopold's American Small Batch Gin (Denver, Colorado) distills each botanical separately, which allows them to capture each aromatic at its optimum temperature and time. They then blend these together for their final product. The count does not have to stop at two; one may blend as many distillates as their heart desires.

Pimm's No. 1 Fruit Cup

There are many spirit-based variations that Pimm's offers today, but it all began in 1840 when James Pimm started serving his Pimm's House Cup, later dubbed Pimm's No. 1 Fruit Cup, in his chain of oyster bars in London. The No. 1 cocktail consists of gin, quinine, closely guarded liqueurs, herbs, and spices served in a pewter pint tankard. The drink became so popular that 19 years later, in 1859, Pimm began bottling his concoction for sale to other establishments. Today it is a British staple, honored as the official drink of the Wimbledon tennis championships and enjoyed by many on a summer's day.

Plymouth Gin

Many debate whether Plymouth is its own category of gin, and there are valid arguments to be had on both sides. Claiming Plymouth as its own genus is not really accurate, but the Black Friars Distillery where it is made does hold a good deal of gin's history in its hands, as they have been producing gin since 1793. It is London's oldest operating distillery—the still has not been changed in over 150 years—and its full-bodied flavor and texture are unique to its locale. The flavor is best exemplified and enhanced by storing the bottle in the freezer prior to making a perfect martini or other tipple.

Those who claim that Plymouth is its own category of gin base their claim on legal proceedings between Plymouth makers, Coates & Co., and other knockoff distilleries that were looking to cash in on the creditability of their name in the 1880s. Coates & Co. were victorious in their suit for exclusive use of the term "Plymouth gin," and it was established that a bottle bearing the title "Plymouth gin" must be produced within Plymouth city. Today, the Plymouth label from Black Friars Distillery is the only Plymouth gin in production. Most spirit-savvy individuals note that they would classify Plymouth gin as a London dry style gin.

The Black Friars Distillery, Plymouth, England.

PECHÉ

208 WEST 4TH STREET
AUSTIN, TEXAS
WWW.PECHEAUSTIN.COM

Austin, Texas, is a town full of life, and even on a 109-degree day like the one that received me, patrons emerge and dart from their air-conditioned retreats to gather and imbibe. Austin has seen its city grow rapidly over the past decade, and there are signs of new construction and restoration throughout the city blocks. Located downtown sits Peché. I enter to find a spacious room with open-beam ceilings high above an expansive wooden bar that lines one side of the room, and large booth seating along the other. Four-bottle-high

Rob Pate.

"A bartender has to relate to people, talk to them, really listen, and keep them entertained."

liquor shelves climb the wall behind the bar and tower over it, accented by elegant paintings of bottles that hang on the surrounding brick wall. I am here to meet Rob Pate, owner and general manager of Peché.

Peché speaks to the pre-Prohibition era when a bartender was a patron's best friend— someone you could count on to make your favorite tipple as well as introduce you to new cocktails. The bartender/client relationship is very important to Rob. I know he classifies bartenders and mixologists as separate terms, prompting me to ask, "Why do you employ 'bartenders' over 'mixologists'? And what, in your

Negroni

1½ oz. sweet vermouth
1½ oz. Campari
1½ oz. gin
Orange twist for garnish

Pour the ingredients into an old-fashioned glass with ice cubes. Stir well. Garnish with orange twist.

Barton Springs

Note: this tastes like a classic dry gin martini.

2 oz. Oxley gin
1 oz. Lillet Blanc
5 drops orange bitters

Stir all ingredients in mixing glass with ice. Strain into chilled martini glass. Garnish with orange twist.

opinion, is the difference?" Rob says, "A bartender has to relate to people, talk to them, really listen, and keep them entertained. A mixologist is often more concerned with the drinks and the performance of drink-making."

"And what makes a good bartender?" I ask. Rob tells me, "First and foremost, our patrons keep our doors open. They keep us in business, and at the end of the day it's about providing a great experience for them. People are lucky to have a lot of options in Austin so we're always fortunate and happy to have guests coming back time and time again. There's a special relationship that builds when you're providing a unique service that, hopefully, makes someone's day better."

I agree, and add, "Austin does have a large bar scene and an emerging gin distillery scene, such as Genius Liquids and Treaty Oak Distilling. When did you first begin to notice that gin was capturing the eye of the craft-distillery movement in Austin?"

"Tito's [vodka] really kicked it off three or four years ago. He was the local guy that made Austin a great launching pad for craft distilleries. Today, we've got gin, bourbon, rum, moonshine, you name it. Tito's put Austin on the map for local distilleries." I thank Rob for his time and reluctantly head back into the heat.

The Bee's Knees

1½ oz. gin
1 tsp. local honey (Peché uses Round Rock honey)
1 tsp. fresh lemon juice
Lemon twist garnish

Combine all ingredients except lemon in a shaker. Shake, strain into a chilled glass, and garnish with lemon twist.

HISTORIC GIN COCKTAILS

I t is an impressive feat, the efficacy with which passing time swallows the accurate recollection of events and facts and leaves only layers of rumors on the plate. Historians, spirit experts, bloggers, and denizens of drinking establishments often debate the cloudy legends that surround the history of libations such as the martini, the Tom Collins, and many others. Such stories have been passed around laxly, many of them cast out from the lubricated lips of those bellied up to the bar amongst comrades. While we may never know the exact circumstances under which some historic cocktails came into fashion, we can be grateful that the rumors remain and that the drinks themselves have endured history's eraser-like footprint and gone on to prosper and inspire.

In today's digital age in which we live, there is an exploding network of history in the making, and, if our descendants have doubts when analyzing our cocktail scene, it will be due to an overabundance of information. And while the veracity of some modern sources remains questionable, there are many reliable records of today's gin productions—photos, tasting notes, production methods, anecdotes, and other bits of relevant info—digitally stored by websites such as www.theginblog.co.uk and www.theginisin.com, that provide vast online databases documenting the new history of gin as we go.

The same cannot be said for unraveling the truth behind the greatest drinks of the past!

One good resource for identifying a cocktail's first historical appearance—and the evidence that many use to support their case—is any bartending book published in or around the years in which the cocktail was rumored to have been established.

Other resources are the stories that are passed down through the years—some highly verifiable, others hearsay—that shape our knowledge of the provenance of classic cocktails.

This section delves into the stories, speculation, and most controversial "facts" behind some of the drinks that carved out their place in culture and paved the way for future generations of fusions. It's a stimulating serving of food for thought to discuss with your comrades the next time you belly up to a bar.

CORPSE REVIVER NO. 2

It wasn't always so frowned upon to have a little libation in the morning, especially after a night of drinking, to alleviate the body's dehydration. In fact, having a cocktail with breakfast was not at all uncommon in pre-Prohibition America and Europe.

You wake up, crack your eyelids, and squint at the light of day. Perhaps you had a bit too much fun last night, and those last few cocktails left you a little parched, aching, and out of focus. It has been historically observed that, while not a recommended remedy, drinking more alcohol the day after generally does improve one's attitude and posture.

The term "corpse reviver," synonymous in drinking circles with the phrase "hair of the dog," is an idiom that denotes any cocktail meant to revitalize the soul and body after a night of significant drinking. At the turn of the nineteenth century, the corpse reviver attached itself to two specific cocktails, No. 1 and then No. 2.

The original corpse reviver No. 1 is brandy-based cocktail and did not follow its successor into popular fashion today. Published in 1870 in London, *The Gentleman's Table*

Corpse Reviver No. 2

1 oz. gin
1 oz. fresh lemon juice
1 oz. Lillet Blanc
1 oz. Cointreau
1 dash absinthe

Build all ingredients in a shaker over ice. Shake and strain into a champagne coupe. May garnish with a lemon peel.

Guide, written by E. Ricket and C. Thomas, describes the corpse reviver's recipe as, "Half wineglass of brandy, half glass of Maraschino, and two dashes of Boker's bitters." Although very different from what would become the No. 2, this appears to be the first written account of a cocktail bearing the title "corpse reviver."

It wasn't until Prohibition drove many American bartenders abroad to practice their trade that many new concoctions came to Europe, thereby stimulating and expanding the cocktail scene. *The Savoy Cocktail Book* (1930) by Harry Craddock contains the first known mention of the corpse reviver No. 2. Craddock had left America and started bartending at the Savoy Hotel in London where he served a wide range of revered cocktails. As Craddock cautions in his book, "four of these taken in swift succession will unrevive the corpse again." It can be said that Craddock is credited with publishing the first known recipe for a corpse reviver No. 2.

For a non-alcoholic concoction and true preventative mixture that's sure to avert the evil curse of the hangover, see Katie Loeb's "A Cautionary Tale" on page 178.

GIN FIZZ
(AND VARIANTS)

There are many variations on the fizz cocktail today, but the classic components of the original are gin, lemon juice, carbonated soda water and sugar, traditionally served in a highball tumbler over ice cubes. Today the fizz family is large, and gin is but one of many options available.

First cited in the 1887 edition of Jerry Thomas' *Bartender's Guide* (alternatively titled *The Bon-Vivant's Companion*), the "fiz" [sic] has become a popular staple and many variations have been fashioned. Even Thomas included six variations in his book. Considered by many to be the "father of American mixology," Thomas went on bartending tours and worked in many cities throughout America and Europe, whipping up and globalizing the popularity of his libations, including the fizz.

As New Orleans approached the twentieth century, the popularity of the gin fizz there began to grow, thanks in part to bartenders such as Henry C. Ramos at the Imperial Cabinet Saloon who made his own variation—the Ramos fizz (or New Orleans fizz). His popular creation, which took a time-consuming 12 minutes to mix, required dozens of bartenders shaking the fizzes to meet demand. Ramos' genuine yet creative take on the fizz consisted of gin, lemon and lime juice, egg white, cream, orange flower water, soda water and sugar, and patrons could not get enough. Word spread throughout the States. *(See the Historic Ramos Gin Fizz cocktail recipe on page 88.)*

Since then, the fizz has grown to be appreciated on an international level in all its variations. One popular gin-based fizz is the sloe gin fizz, which employs sloe gin either as a substitution or an addition to a dry gin. Regardless of the variation being employed, historically many bartenders have put extra care and effort into creating a fizz. For example, *The Gentleman's Companion* (Charles H. Baker, Jr., 1939) gives a glimpse into a fizz called the Aziz Special, which was served at Egypt's Winter Palace Hotel.

Today we are seeing even more creative fizz concoctions at venues far and wide, such as Amis in Philadelphia which offers a rosemarino gin fizz containing Plymouth sloe gin, limoncello, and fresh rosemary.

Gin Fizz

2 oz. gin
3-4 oz. soda water
Juice of ½ lemon
½ tsp. sugar or simple syrup

Build ingredients, sans club soda, in a shaker over ice. Shake and strain into a tumbler glass over ice. Top with soda water.

Aziz Special Gin Fizz

From *The Gentleman's Companion, Volume II, Being an Exotic Drinking Book* (Charles H. Baker Jr., 1939):

"Put 1 to 1½ tsp. of sugar into the shaker, add 2 jiggers of dry or Old Tom gin—to preference—the juice of 1 small lemon, 1 pony of thick cream and 1 tbsp. of fresh egg white. Put in lots of finely cracked ice, shake hard and long, turn into a big goblet leaving a few ice lumps floating. Add 2 or 3 good dashes of orange flower water. Now fill up with chilled Number 1 grade club soda. Stir once. Serve immediately and drink soon, thereafter, since no gin fizz gains virtue even from brief neglect."

GIN AND TONIC

Although it may seem that the gin and tonic, or G&T, is a simple, self-explanatory highball, there are almost endless variations being served up by today's top cocktail makers. Innovative venues such as New York City's Gin Palace have blasted through the legal red tape to bring you G&Ts on tap. They also provide guests with a choice of tonics to compliment the varieties of gin they offer—such as a "three-pepper" tonic combined with Aviation gin.

At the London Gin Club in England, members can rejoice at the large selection of garnishes that have been specifically paired with each of the gins. The variables one has to choose from when selecting the perfect combination include the gin label, the brand of tonic, the accoutrements or garnishes, the form of ice, and sometimes the addition of other flavors such as bitters. Although the gin and tonic has risen in popularity recently as a refreshing summer cocktail in America and Spain, its beginnings came about in an entirely practical fashion.

Soldiers of the British East India Company made the first gin and tonic in the early nineteenth century, primarily to fend off malaria. Quinine,

Gin and Tonic

2 oz. gin
4 oz. tonic water
1 lime wedge (US)
1 lemon wedge (UK)

Place cracked or cubed ice in a
highball glass. Combine gin and
tonic water. Stir and garnish.

found in the bark of the cinchona tree, was known to prevent contraction of malaria. Due to the fact that quinine is naturally bitter, soldiers made it more palatable by mixing it with water, citric acid (lemon or lime juice), sugar, and gin.

In 1870 the Schweppes Company, the same manufacturer still producing tonic today, brought their Indian Quinine Tonic to market. And by the latter part of that century, the availability of prepared tonic water gave rise to a boom in gin and tonics in Britain and her colonies.

BOUQUET

DIXIE BELLE Dry Gin has that most desirable of social attributes — the ability to mingle without ostentation. It is a suave, smooth gin, of delicate yet definite bouquet — agreeably smooth, superbly dry — a real contribution to post-Repeal mixing. To you who demand a gin of really distinguished merit, Continental dedicates this fine, dry gin — distilled for your pleasure — and identified by this seal — "Distilled by Continental."

Also distillers of Envoy Club, Snug Harbor and Sweep Stakes Blended Whiskies, and Cavalier Distilled Dry Gin.

This advertisement is not intended to offer alcoholic beverages for sale or delivery in any state wherein the sale or use thereof is unlawful.

Distilled by CONTINENTAL DISTILLING CORP., Philadelphia

Vintage ad from the 1930s.

THE MARTINI
(AND VARIATIONS)

Martini

2–3 oz. quality gin
Quality vermouth, to taste (from
none to 3 oz.)
Lemon peel, or lemon oil from
zest, or olive garnish
Optional orange bitters (popular
until the 1950s)

Combine gin, vermouth, and bitters
in a mixer over ice. Either shake or
stir until the outside of the shaker
is frosted. Strain into a martini
glass. May garnish with a twist of
lemon, or simply a drop of fresh
lemon oil from zest, or an olive.
*(Note: There are so many amazing
martinis available from today's
pioneering mixologists, but this
recipe is safe and classic. It is the
base.)*

The martini, possibly the most
notorious of all gin potions, is
no longer simply a cocktail. It
is a symbol, an indication of
sophistication, refinement, and
most evidently a love of gin. The
variations on the martini are
boundless, and while today some
bars will call just about anything
in a v-shaped glass a martini, it is
not so. Whatever your conviction,
for the purposes of this dialog,
vodka and other less-than-classic
variations will be omitted.

What makes the perfect martini?
Shaken or stirred? Olives or lemon
peel? Perfect, dry, or extra-dry? This
is a subject of heated debate based
on personal palates and historical
associations. One popular semi-
modern practice is to remove ice
from the martini equation entirely.
It is generally agreed, in lieu of an
official tasting, that most prefer
gin's notes at a crisp temperature.
Although James Bond made it
cool, and everyone likes to see a
bartender furiously undulating a
shaker above his or her head, the
advent of refrigeration killed the

need to shake a martini, or even use ice, to chill the liquid. If you walk into Harry's Bar in Venice, Italy, do not expect to hear any shaking coming from behind the bar. Both glass and premixed martini cocktail are drawn from a freezer. (For a deeper look, see the feature with Arrigo Cipriani of Harry's Bar on page 124.) On the other hand, some say that the reason to shake a martini is so that tiny flakes of ice break off and melt, stimulating and releasing the aromatics on a molecular level and bringing the gin to life. The stirrer's rebuttal is that stirring or swirling gin in ice produces melt as well, while using a more controlled method that doesn't bruise the gin.

So where did the martini come from and how did it evolve? There are many opinions and few facts when it comes to answering this historically vague question. Perhaps the historians were taking respite at the bar enjoying one for a brief moment. Some claim its name was inspired by the late nineteenth-century British rifle—the Martini-Henry—which was known for its intense recoil. There is not much substance behind this claim besides the name association. Others place the credit with Italian vermouth producer Martini & Rossi, who at one point in the late nineteenth century is said to have bottled and sold a popular pre-mixed blend of gin and their vermouth under the label Martini. This does appear to hold some weight,

THE DIRTY MARTINI & THE GIBSON

For those who need a little distraction in their martini, ask for a *dirty* martini (or a martini with olive juice in it) for a pleasant adaptation. One trick of the trade is to use less olive juice, but place the olives in the bottom of the martini glass before serving from the shaker. Swirling all the alcohol through and around the olives brings out their flavor and steals it away into the juice. The gibson's name makes it sound like it is worlds away from a martini, but in truth the only difference is the garnish. Replace the martini's garnish with a cocktail onion and it transforms into a gibson. The pickled vinegar essence of the onion definitely contributes to differentiating the gibson from the martini.

but still lacks supporting documents to prove invention. Martini & Rossi was also responsible for taking an initial risk by distributing their dry vermouth to the United States, an act that paid off big for them and would change American cocktails forever.

Another claim is that it wasn't until vermouth made its way to New York City's Knickerbocker Hotel and fell into the hands of bartender Martini di Arma di Taggia (yes, his name was actually Martini), that the true martini was born in America. Preceding dry vermouth's importation to the States, there were several sweeter drinks—such as the fancy gin cocktail, harmonizing Old Tom gin and orange curacao—which were popular and are historically significant as they preceded the martini's invention.

It does seem clear that the Martinez cocktail preceded the martini. It held some resemblance to a martini but was much sweeter and used Old Tom gin instead of London dry. The Martinez is first mentioned in O.H. Byron's *Modern Bartender's Guide* (1884). Byron writes toward the bottom of a page dedicated to manhattan cocktail variations, under the heading Martinez, "Same as Manhattan, only you substitute gin for whisky." Soon after, American Jerry Thomas released his 1887 edition of the *Bartender's Guide*, also including a Martinez recipe.

Ultimately, it is generally agreed upon that the first written mention of a cocktail actually called a martini was in Harry Johnson's second edition of his *Bartender Manual* (1888).

Just like most areas of humanity, the evolutionary path of most cocktails is not always clear-cut, and there's not always just one passageway to the truth. Similar trends and progressions occur simultaneously in unconnected regions all over the world. Global tastes shift as people experiment, travel, connect, and interact. Most likely the martini was born, like many of its siblings, from investigating and modifying the cocktails that came before it.

O.H. Byron's 1884 Martinez

½ wine-glass [1 oz.] gin
½ wine-glass [1 oz.] Italian vermouth
2 dashes [¼ oz.] Curacoa
2 dashes Angostura bitters
1 orange-twist garnish

Combine all liquid ingredients in a mixer over ice. Stir well and strain into a cocktail glass. Garnish with an orange twist.

WHISKEY SOUR

2 OZ. WHISKEY
1 TSP. POWDERED SUGAR
JUICE ½ LEMON & ½ LIME
SHAKE WITH CRACKED ICE
STRAIN, AND SERVE

MARTINI

⅔ DRY GIN
⅓ FRENCH VERMOUTH
DASH ORANGE BITTERS
STIR WITH CRACKED ICE
SERVE WITH AN OLIVE

GIN & TONIC

1 JIGGER GIN
INDIAN QUININE WATER
POUR GIN ADD ICE
SLICE LEMON OR LIME
ADD MIXER SERVE

THE FAMOUS HARRY'S
BAR MARTINI
WITH ARRIGO CIPRIANI

CALLE VALLARESSO, 1323
VENEZIA, ITALY
WWW.CIPRIANI.COM

There are just some places that make you feel alive. Venice, Italy, the sinking city, is one of them. It inspires with its soft-spoken canals veining through city blocks, the sounds of pigeons taking to the air while you stroll through St. Mark's Square, and most pertinent of all, its cocktail history. Many great thinkers and artists at one time called Venice home. Those such as Giovanni Bellini, Casanova, Marco Polo, Antonio Vivaldi, and F. Scott Fitzgerald all made stays in Venice. In addition to all the personalities, Venice holds Harry's Bar. There's something special about drinking the same cocktail that Hemingway held to his lips in the exact same bar decades earlier; it makes you smile.

> "Bartenders dressed in white coats and black bowties welcome me and offer a seat at the bar. I know what I'm there for—the famous martini cocktail."

I walk up to Harry's Bar, which rests on the corner of a block that ends at the water of St. Mark's Bay, and stop to watch the gondolas cut through the canal with an assassin's prowess. As I enter, bartenders dressed in

white coats and black bowties welcome me and offer a seat at the bar. I know what I'm there for—the famous martini cocktail. Pulled straight from the freezer and into a glass, my martini is served with precise execution. As I sip my frozen martini I can't help but think about the others who have drank here in the past—Orson Welles, Charlie Chaplin, Truman Capote, Aristotle Onassis, and Alfred Hitchcock, to name but a few. The atmosphere feels inspirational, yet I am not inspired to the point of attempting to set up an impromptu meeting. I take notes, enjoy the martini and think about my future correspondence. A month after visiting Harry's I reached out with the hopes of speaking with someone about their martini.

I could not have been more thrilled when my attempt to enlist Harry's Bar in *The Spirit of Gin* resulted in the following emailed response:

"I am Arrigo Cipriani, born in 1931, in attendance of Harry's Bar nearly every day since 1950. I am the son of Giuseppe who opened it in 1931. As the man responsible of the Dry Martini you have experienced, I guess I am the person you would like to get in touch with. . . . Looking forward to hearing from you."

I couldn't believe it—the man himself had replied. Not only that, but Mr. Cipriani graciously agreed to allow publication of his family's famous martini recipe for the first time (to my knowledge) in an English-language book; it had been printed in the Italian book, *Prisoner in a Room in Venice*, as excerpted (and translated) below:

> *For the sake of my readers, and for their happiness, I've decided to hand over my dry Martini recipe.*
>
> *The easiest of all the cocktails, but also the most refined one.*
>
> *The ingredients are:*
>
> *Gin, which for me is Gordon's. Always Gordon's, in my opinion, and dry vermouth. Among all the dry vermouths, I prefer Martini dry.*
>
> *The quantities for 10 persons are:*
>
> *730 g [25¾ oz.] of gin*
>
> *20 g [nearly ¾ oz.] of dry vermouth*
>
> *The cooking pot is a good freezer.*
>
> *For the sake of simplicity, from now on I will simply call "Martini" the Martini cocktail.*
>
> *Let me start by saying that Martini has the only dry taste that exists in the world. It is not sweet, nor bitter, nor sour, nor salty. It is dry. Therefore, the Martini MUST be dry. The only purpose of the vermouth is to remove the light juniper taste from the gin, but one should not be aware of its presence.*
>
> *That explains the minimum quantity of vermouth needed, compared to the gin.*
>
> *Another essential characteristic of the Martini is that it must be served frozen.*
>
> *Before the invention of the freezer, the ice was the only comfort.*
>
> *The Martini stirred with ice (never shaken!) was therefore cold, even glacial, but it could never be frozen. It was served in*

stemmed glasses, because the stem prevented the warmth of the fingers from heating the liquid.

After the invention of the freezer, stemmed glasses are no longer necessary. The perfect glass is the 60 grams (2 oz.) cylindrical one.

When the preparation is done, the gin bottle must always be kept in the freezer. And so the glasses.

Attention now!

The recipe should be prepared with gin and vermouth at room temperature.

Directions:

1. Pour 20 grams [2 oz.] of gin out of the bottle and give it to the human being next to you. Usually he will not ask why.

2. Pour 20 grams [2 oz.] of vermouth into the gin bottle. Cap the bottle back again and turn it over a couple of times. Then store it in the freezer.

3. When the temperature of the bottle reaches 0 Fahrenheit, the Martini is ready to be served. Just fill one of the frozen glasses, close your eyes and try it.

You are tasting the best Martini of your life.

Ice is not required because it would only contribute to dilute the nectar.

Everything else does not matter. Olives, baby onions, zest, lemon twist, are nothing but deceptions to make an ordinary Martini taste like a good one. . . .

On the table inside my pyramid I would like a bottle of Gordon's Gin and one of Vermouth dry Martini. I am sure I will share them with Giunone, one time or another.

A NIGHT IN THE DISTRICT
WITH DEREK BROWN

WASHINGTON, DC

Feeling good after tasting three varieties of Green Hat gin at New Columbia Distillers, I arrive in front of Mockingbird Hill, a new restaurant and bar with a focus on great sherry, to meet with owner Derek Brown, who has numerous successful venues in the District of Columbia and also does a good deal of writing about cocktails, bar-side manner, and other pertinent subjects.

Derek Brown.

I am a little early for our meeting, but I wander in. Derek, an entrepreneur, restaurateur, and cocktail and music lover, greets me and immediately pours me a glass of sherry before taking me to the back room where a small class is being held on cured meats. There's a sign on the wall that proclaims: "Cured Wednesdays 5pm-6pm." After being schooled on some amazing cured varieties, Derek invites me to join him at the front bar where they have a gin and tonic on tap. Yes, on tap. It is made with locally distilled Green Hat gin and a house-made tonic. A dried slice of apple rests on top of a large house-made ice cube. I never

The Passenger.

found out what went into their tonic, but the orange tint of the cocktail, and the unique and delectable taste, convey to me that a good deal of thought went into it.

I overhear Derek alerting the bartender that the music is a new playlist he is working on that consists of bands from the District, but it is not complete yet, and to make sure the room doesn't go silent. Being a musician myself, I am immediately impressed by his attention to detail and the thought that he puts into creating the right atmosphere for all his venues.

We then walk next door to Derek's current labor of love, two new bars that share a kitchen. One, dubbed Eat the Rich, will be an oyster bar and the other, unnamed to date, will be a southern bourbon bar. It is apparent that the block is going through a transformation, and Derek's commitment to open three unique bars on it speaks to his commitment to the District.

After finishing our cocktails we head to the metro, venturing toward the Passenger, a bar that also serves food and is co-owned and operated by Derek's brother, Tom. It's about 7:30 p.m. by the time we arrive; the bar is already hopping and the music is kicking. Derek introduces me to his brother behind the bar who proceeds to make me a delicious gin-based variation on a zombie cocktail.

Just as I'm beginning to think the night is wrapping up, Derek looks at me and says, "But you haven't seen the Columbia Room yet. You really should at least *taste* the martini." I agree and, without even realizing where I am going, we slip through an unpronounced passage in the back of the Passenger to a dimly lit small bar, a bar within a bar. The room is beautiful and it feels like I'm in a secret society as I sit there. This is the place where politicians and the like come to enjoy privacy and an amazing martini.

Many have praised the martini they serve, and I carefully watch the bartender put great time and detail into its crafting. The process begins by removing a bottle of Plymouth gin and a glass from a freezer. Then out comes the bottle of Dolan dry vermouth. With a jigger, equal parts vermouth and gin are combined over ice and stirred. The next step, which I have never seen before, is the thermometer reading. After stirring, the bartender places it into the shaker and awaits the reading. "It has to be exactly the correct temperature," she tells me, "a cool 29 degrees." Upon achieving the desired temperature, the juice is strained into our martini glasses. Two fresh peels of lemon are sliced artfully but not placed in our glasses. Instead she simply cracks the peel above the drink allowing a drop of lemon essence to fall into the cocktail. "This way you get the lemon essence without all the bitterness," Derek tells me. She places two gray felt coasters on the bar and sets our drinks in front of us. "Cheers!"

> "Although olives complement the martini, they do not actually belong *in* the drink. Much better on the side."

I have to say, it may just be the best martini I have ever had. Derek explains to me how freezing the gin is important because it changes its texture, thickening it, and that Plymouth is exceptionally receptive to this. He's right. Texturally it is perfect. We receive some Spanish olives on the side, as Derek tells me, "Although olives complement the martini, they do not actually belong *in* the drink. Much better on the side." Having reached my quota of alcohol I can consume in an evening, I thank Derek and find my way back to the Metro.

PERCURSORS TO THE MARTINI

By Derek Brown

1700 BC-476 AD: In classical antiquity, flavored wine is mixed at precise ratios (e.g. 2:1) with water at symposiums. It's considered a point of pride to mix well.

8th century: Distillation emerges from Arab culture, beginning with its discovery by alchemist Abu Musa Jabir ibn Hayyan (Geber).

11th century: Juniper wine is used as a medicine at the world's most prestigious medical school in Salerno, Italy.

15th century: Juniper brandy appears in Holland.

18th century: Vermouth is given its name in Italy by Antonia Benedetto Carpano from the German word for wormwood, "vermut."

19th century: Both dry gin and dry vermouth appear in Britain and France, respectively.

Late 19th century: Dry martini appears under mysterious origins, sometimes erroneously linked to Jerry Thomas or Martini & Rossi vermouth. Some precursors to the dry martini as we know it include:

1884: The Martinez. It is quite possible that the Martinez was based on the manhattan, substituting gin for whiskey.

1888: The Martine. Mistakenly labeled as "The Martine" in an illustration in Harry Johnson's *New and Improved Illustrated Bartender's Manual or How to Mix Drinks of the Present Style*, this is the first printed mention of the word "Martini."

1895: The Turf Club. No vermouth, but same basic principle with a little extra bitters. From George J. Kappeler's *Modern American Drinks*. Old Tom gin with a dash of Angostura and three dashes orange bitters.

1896: The Margueritte. This is the earliest written recipe for the dry martini in Thomas Stuart's *Stuart's Fancy Drinks and How to Mix Them*. Close enough to the name martini, the name "Margueritte" was easily absorbed.

1900: The Puritan (2:1). Very close to the Margueritte, this one calls for Yellow Chartreuse. The recipe appears alongside the martini in Fredrick L. Knowles' *The Cocktail Book: A Sideboard Manual for Gentlemen*.

TOM COLLINS

The origin story of the Tom Collins has been crowded with many declarations and claims. As history propels and new information comes to light, it is still difficult to discern the one complete and accurate story. Mixologist, historian, and author David Wondrich recently brought a 1904 article to light which toppled previous theories and provides a current leading viewpoint. Nevertheless, it is worthwhile to hear each theory.

One popular claim held that the cocktail originated from John Collins, a bartender who served a gin punch at Limmer's Hotel in 1820s and 1830s London, which may very well have been a predecessor to the Tom Collins. The punch initially used oude genever, a style of the Dutch forerunner to gin. A little experimentation soon produced a cocktail where Old Tom gin replaced genever, hence a "Tom Collins."

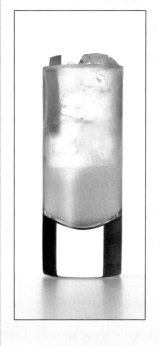

Tom Collins

2 oz. Old Tom gin
¾ oz. fresh lemon juice (may use lime juice and orange juice in addition)
2 sugar cubes
2 oz. soda water
Cherry and a lemon-peel or orange-peel garnish

Build gin, lemon juice, and sugar in a shaker over ice. Shake and strain into a Collins glass. Top with soda water. Garnish. Experiment with blending lime, orange, and lemon juices in place of just lemon juice, keeping the ¾ oz. proportion. (Note: Many modern recipes use London dry gin instead of Old Tom, which is not historically accurate. If you don't have Old Tom gin but want a sweet cocktail, try adding a third sugar cube with the London dry.)

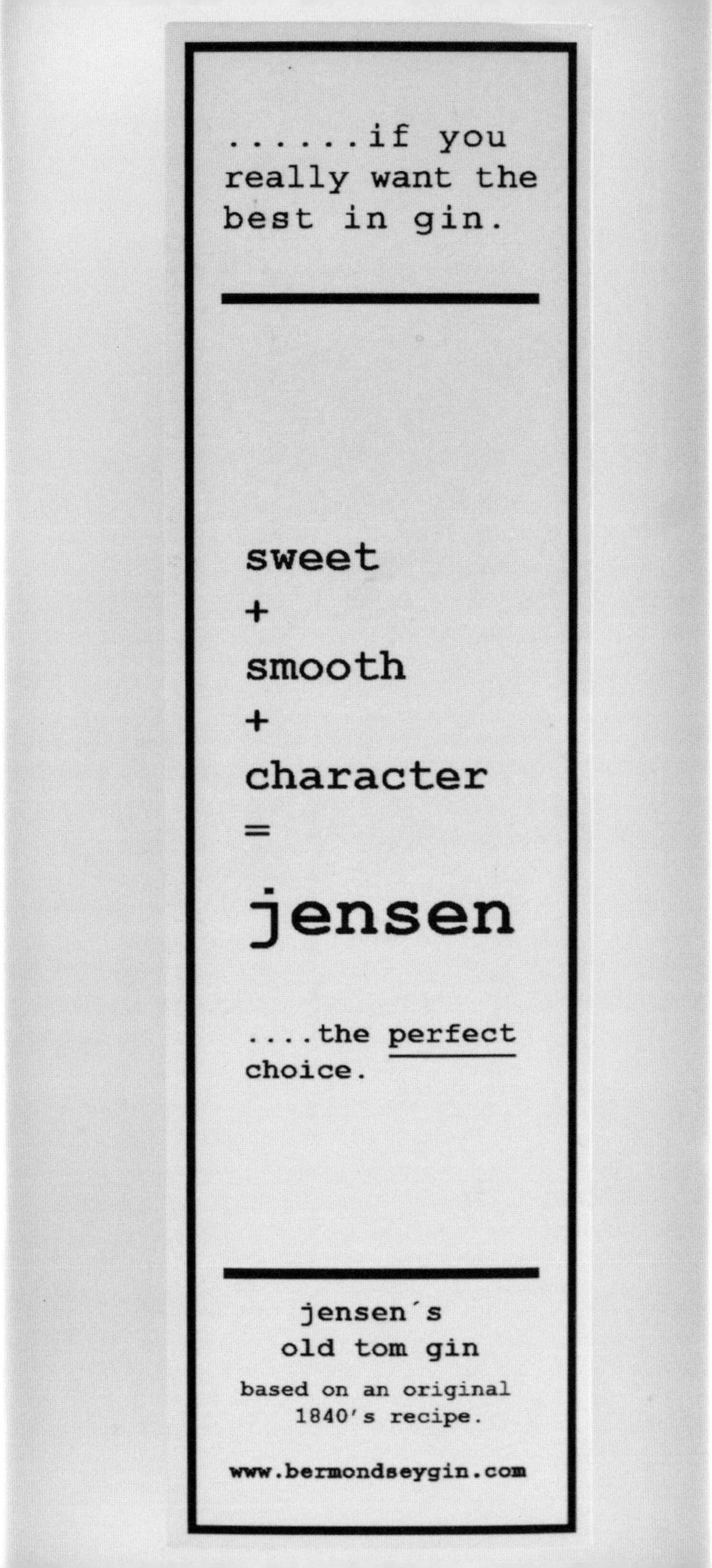

......if you
really want the
best in gin.

---

sweet
+
smooth
+
character
=

jensen

....the perfect
choice.

---

jensen's
old tom gin

based on an original
1840's recipe.

www.bermondseygin.com

There are also a few historical mentions that credit an American, Stephen Price, living in London and working at the Garrick Club around the same time, although this appears to be a minority opinion (at least via documentation). It has been said that Price was not the most charismatic fellow, and that perhaps history did what it does best and forgot that which was not recorded.

Others believe the Tom Collins cocktail received its name from "The Great Tom Collins Hoax of 1874." The "hoax" was in fact a prank that rose to popularity in Philadelphia and New York. Basically, one would tell one's friend that a fellow named Tom Collins was spreading nasty rumors about him at the local tavern. The person being pranked would then go looking for the man in the tavern by name. The prank is described in the following excerpt from an article that appeared in the *Gettysburg Compiler* of 1874:

Have You Seen Tom Collins?

If you haven't, perhaps you had better do so, and as quick as you can, for he is talking about you in a very rough manner— calling you hard names, and altogether saying things about you that are rather calculated to induce people to believe there is nothing you wouldn't steal short of a red-hot stove. Other little things of that nature he is openly speaking in public places, and as a friend—although of course we don't wish to make you feel uncomfortable—we think you ought to take some notice of them and of Mr. Tom Collins.

This is about the cheerful substance of a very successful practical joke which has been going the rounds of the city in the past week. It is not to this manor born, but belongs to New York, where it was played with immense success to crowded houses until it played out.

Amidst all the confusion the prank had generated, an observant bartender decided to create a cocktail and name it "Tom Collins." The next person who strolled into their bar asking for "Tom Collins" would have just unintentionally purchased a cocktail! The prank became extremely popular and soon was too well-known to pull off.

Some credit America with the invention of the Tom Collins, and claim the cocktail found its way to Europe as bartenders traveled overseas during Prohibition. To date, the first known written mention of a Tom Collins comes from Jerry Thomas' 1877 printing of his *Bon Vivant's Companion*.

The most recent uncovered documents, found and publicized by David Wondrich, were in the form of a 1904 magazine article that stated the following of the "John" Collins punch: "This world-renowned beverage, still popular in America, and not forgotten on this side of the Atlantic, was compounded of gin, soda water, ice, lemon and sugar."

The mention does not specify what type of gin, but that's the fundamental recipe for a Tom, or a John, Collins. It is reasonable to deduct that the Tom Collins is a derivative of the John Collins, and that even if a form of the Tom Collins gained popularity in America in the late nineteenth century—which then, in turn, brought back its prominence to Europe during US Prohibition—the first Tom Collins-esque cocktail seems to have been served in London. Still, there are no absolutes.

THE WHITE LADY

Some cocktails' origins have been spun by time, but the white lady, also known as a Delilah cocktail, appears to have a somewhat distinct history. It all starts with Harry MacElhone, who began working at Harry's New York Bar in Paris around 1920 after developing a stellar reputation crafting cocktails at Ciro's Club in London. The white lady first appears in print in Harry Craddock's *Savoy Cocktail Book* (1930).

The original white lady differs from what it came to be and how it is known today. MacElhone had previously made a similar cocktail using crème de menthe in place of gin, ordered as a white lady. Upon arriving in Paris, he had a revelation that inspired him to modify that incredibly unhealthy, outlandishly sweet drink into something new and interesting. Something, in fact, that would catch on. MacElhone replaced the crème de menthe with gin and reduced the amount of Cointreau, and the white

Pink Lady

1½ oz. gin
½ oz. fresh lemon juice
½ oz. applejack or apple brandy
(some include this ingredient,
some do not)
2 dashes grenadine
1 fresh egg white
Maraschino cherry garnish

Build all ingredients (except garnish) over ice in a shaker. Shake and strain into a chilled cocktail glass. Garnish. (Note: The pink lady is less popular today because it unfairly gained a reputation as a weak cocktail. It is actually a fine cocktail that deserves to be brought back into fashion.)

White Lady

1½ oz. gin
¾ oz. Cointreau
¾ oz. fresh lemon juice
½ fresh egg white (optional)

Combine all ingredients in shaker over ice. Shake strongly to froth the egg white and chill. Strain into a cocktail glass.

lady was born. Hemingway actually mentions the white lady in his novel *Islands in the Stream* (published posthumously in 1970). MacElhone's new interpretation of the white lady took off and is still commonplace on bar menus today.

WISDOM

Erik Holzherr is a great guy. With the book's deadline rapidly approaching he invited me to one of his venues, Wisdom, to discuss gin and allow me to further my education one last time. What led me to Erik was a website he runs dubbed www.gintender.com, where he discusses his love of gin, gin-related news, and events at his venues. I drove from Philadelphia to Washington, DC, to meet the man and join a private cocktail class he was hosting at Wisdom.

> "Vodka, to me, is boring. . . . It's never going to accentuate a drink."

Upon entering, the atmospheric decor is a combination of soft wooden warmth and original exposed brick. The bar is up front to my left, presenting shelves packed with gin, vermouth, and various other bottles. I introduce myself to Erik and he encourages me to take a look around. Past the bar is a calm living-room lounge setup, with tapestries on the walls and a chandelier that hangs over couches and chairs and secondary seating recesses.

While my excitement for the group lesson grows, I quickly realize my good fortune when the whole class, prepaid no less, doesn't show. I now have Erik's full attention. Slowly the bar that had been occupied by just a few patrons

Erik Holzherr.

Wisdom.

Eminent Domaine (Wisdom)

1 oz. of Bluecoat gin
¾ oz. of Domaine de Canton
ginger cognac liqueur
¼ oz. Luxardo Amaro
¾ oz. pressed apple juice
¼ oz. fresh squeezed lime

Combine all ingredients in a shaker
over ice. Shake and strain into
a martini glass.

begins to fill up. A friendly British couple walks up and claims the two barstools to my right. They know Erik, and we all begin chatting. Nicki and Steven Sullivan are not gin fans, and that makes an excellent setup for Erik to work his magic. As we talk about the English perception of gin, they tell me one difference abroad was that in their experience, mainly as witness to their parents, gin and tonics were garnished with a lemon wedge, not lime. Although they had obviously been to Wisdom before, it didn't seem as

Absolution (Wisdom)

1 ½ oz. Plymouth gin
¾ oz. Yellow Chartreuse liqueur
1 oz. Dubonnet Blanc
1 oz. pressed apple juice
1 brandied white grape garnish*

Shake all ingredients together with ice and strain into a wine glass, mist with Cointreau, and add garnish. (*Soak de-stemmed grape for at least 3–4 days in Green Chartreuse.)

if they had heard Erik explain why gin is his favorite spirit.

He begins, "When it comes to mixing gin and vodka, vodka's going to disappear, right? Vodka, to me, is boring because of that. It's never going to accentuate a drink. If you mix gin correctly, you're getting trace elements. In most gins you're putting the botanicals in and you're distilling them. So you're getting trace elements, you're getting the essential oils, subtle elements—botanicals on the tongue that are hard to distinguish. When you mix it appropriately with different things, those essences can pop and accentuate a drink, where vodka will never do that. Vodka will always disappear." Consequently Nicki ordered a martini upon Erik's recommendation. (See Erik's feature, *How to Convert a Vodka Drinker to a Gin Sipper*, on page 206.)

Chuck Yeager (Church & State)

Our all-American tweak of the Aviation cocktail.
1½ oz. Leopold's gin
¾ oz. Leopold Michigan tart cherry liqueur
½ a lemon's fresh-squeezed juice
1 dash lavender bitters

Shake all ingredients with ice and strain into a coupe glass, add a dash of lavender bitters.

LEOPOLD'S
AMERICAN SMALL BATCH GIN

BATCH NO. 1212

We distill each batch of gin from only the finest botanicals including juniper and orris root, as well as hand-zested American pummelos and oranges. Each handcrafted batch is unique, yielding only fifty cases of an exceptionally complex yet subtle spirit which both those new to American gin and the connoisseur will appreciate. - Todd Leopold, Master Distiller

750ml, 80 Proof, 40% Alc. by Vol.

Envy (Church & State)

½ oz. Bluecoat gin
½ oz. Leopold maraschino cherry liqueur
½ oz. house-made grenadine*
1 orange twist garnish

Shake all ingredients with ice and strain into a martini glass.
Add an orange twist garnish. (*House-made grenadine is 50%
fresh-squeezed pomegranate juice and 50% simple syrup.)

Erik tells me that for higher-proof gins, he likes to shake a cocktail to
lower the proof slightly and make its botanicals distinguishable and have
less burn. To clarify, he adds, "You're not drinking any less alcohol."

We chat about Church & State, another venue Erik owns that only uses
American products, especially Leopold Brother's (Denver, Colorado) line of
labels, which are crafted exclusively from American elements. In addition,
Church & State make their own vermouth, grenadine, ginger beer, and
tonic. Erik tells me about a bottle his staff bought him to celebrate his bar's
four-year anniversary, which he still can't bring himself to open. It's a bottle
of Nolet Reserve, "The most expensive gin in history," Erik says, clocking in
at $699 per bottle. I thank Erik for his time.

Right: The art of the pour.

AUXILIARY
LIQUIDS

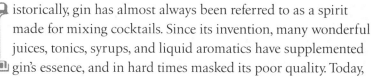

Historically, gin has almost always been referred to as a spirit made for mixing cocktails. Since its invention, many wonderful juices, tonics, syrups, and liquid aromatics have supplemented gin's essence, and in hard times masked its poor quality. Today, gin's splendor rests in the vast quantities of both traditional and forward-looking spirits being produced. To supplement this growth, house-made tonics, bitters, boutique vermouths, and other fresh juices regularly line the bar, ready to provide inspiration to the creative mixologist.

Tonics

One-half of the celebrated gin and tonic cocktail, tonic is the underdog that has the talent to make or break the union. It is just as essential as the gin when mixing a craft cocktail, as is the quality of any ingredient.

The primary flavoring agent in tonic is quinine, made from the bark of the cinchona tree. While the tree's bark has been known for its medicinal qualities since the sixteenth century, tonic water came into fashion in the early nineteenth century amongst the malaria-stricken British East India Company. The medicine, in its simplest historical form, was taken by adding cut-and-sifted cinchona bark to genever and letting it rest for five to six days. These potions had much higher quinine content and were mixed with sugar and water to cut the bitterness. Tonic water soon was being made as a standalone mixer to be combined with gin as needed. Today, there is a wide array of tonic brands that utilize supplemental ingredients such as lemongrass, citrus fruits, allspice, citric acid, cardamom, and other aromatics.

In the United States many assume there are no other options besides Schweppes, Seagrams, and Canada Dry, but this is incorrect. Some newer tonics have hit the US market giving customers a variety of quality tonics to choose from for a premium price. Some lesser-known varieties now available are Q Tonic, Fever Tree, Fentimans, and White Rock. Bittermens Spirits, located in New Orleans, produces Commonwealth Tonic Liqueur, which may be used in place of tonic water in conjunction with club soda. The remedy contains alcohol, allowing Bittermens to capture a more sophisticated

Tab. 375.

Cinchona officinalis. L.

quinine essence, which results in a less sweet, complexly bitter tonic. Alcohol can absorb botanicals' essences in a way that water cannot. There is a serious distinction between quality tonics and those that use quinine flavoring and high-fructose corn syrup to manufacture their products. Trying a new craft tonic can totally transform a cocktail, and it doesn't have to be a G&T. Other lesser-known cocktails that include both tonic water and gin include the gin lime rickey, the classy bitch, and the Campari safari.

Much of tonic's history is closely tied to gin. See the Gin and Tonic feature on page 115 for the larger story.

FEVER TREE TONIC

Fever Tree, produced in London, offers several varieties of carbonates including Indian, Mediterranean, lemon, ginger beer, and naturally light tonics. Their superb ginger beer combines especially well with gin, such as Tanqueray 10. The Indian tonic uses soft spring water and high-quality quinine, harvested from the fever tree, a nickname for the cinchona tree, on a plantation in the Congo. Besides quinine, the Mediterranean tonic utilizes lemon oils from Sicily, lemon thyme and rosemary from Provence, geranium, and mandarin. It is finely carbonated and its bubbles are small, on par with champagne. This creates a very round flavor and smooth sip. Fever Tree is available at some specialty shops in the United States, and its reputation here is slowly catching up to the esteem it has across the Atlantic.

FEVER-TREE
Premium Natural Mixers

SYRUPS

Syrups can really invigorate a cocktail and are a useful addition to any professional or home bar. By creating their own auxiliary liquids, a bar can become something special and unique. Most syrups may be made with the addition of infusing herbs, fruits, and spices into the basic simple syrup recipe. Lemon, honey, cardamom, ginger, lavender, rosemary, and vanilla syrups are all good options to begin experimenting with. Inviting friends over for gin and tonics and surprising them with your own homemade tonic syrup will unequivocally delight and

Simple Syrup Recipe

The basic ratio for simple syrup is one part sugar to one part water. Some make rich simple syrup, which combines two parts sugar to one part water and reduces the amount needed in cocktail recipes. You may use white granulated sugar, or brown sugar for a more historical flavor and aesthetic. If using brown sugar, run it through a food processor once to break up the granules and help them to dissolve. You may also add gum syrup (gum acacia or gum Arabia) to thicken the syrup, producing a smoother texture.

Directions: Heat the water in a pot on the stove at the lowest possible temperature. Slowly add portions of the sugar, stirring until the sugar dissolves between additions. Once all the sugar is dissolved, let it cool, then bottle.

Make Your Own Tonic Syrup

Although it may seem demanding, making your own homemade tonic syrup is actually a fairly simple process. And it is worth it. A tonic made with all-natural, organic ingredients yields a superior taste. When trying your hand at syrup production, do not be timid about altering this base recipe with additional ingredients and experimenting. Depending on what cocktails you plan on making with your tonic, you can try infusing citrus and botanicals such as lavender, mint, elderflower, orange peel, allspice berries, and lemon peel. Some add a pinch of good kosher or sea salt.

For the base recipe, you will need:

4 cups water
3 cups cane sugar or agave
6 tbsp. citric acid powder
3 tbsp. cinchona bark powder
3 limes (zest and juice)
1 cup chopped lemongrass stalk

Combine water and sugar or agave in a medium saucepan, bring to a boil, and stir. Once the sugar is dissolved, turn the heat to low. Add the citric acid, cinchona bark, lime zest, lime juice, and lemongrass to the saucepan and stir. Let simmer for 20–30 minutes until all powder is dissolved. Remove from heat and let cool. Pour the liquid through a strainer to first remove the larger solids. You may also use a French coffee press to remove the bark and other solids. Then use a cheesecloth or some coffee filters to finely purify the syrup. This will require patience. Bottle it in an airtight jar and store in the fridge. For most cocktails, adding a few tablespoons of syrup to four ounces of soda water is a good start.

Don't be surprised when the result is not the clear liquid you are used to seeing. The yellowish brown hue comes from using real cinchona bark and not synthetic quinine. Cinchona bark, which is used to produce quinine powder, may be purchased at many local herb shops and from online retailers such as www.dandelionbotanical.com and www.healthyvillage.com.

impress. There are also syrup brands on the market for instant satisfaction. Companies such as Bittermens, Daily's, Davinci Gourmet, Tomr's, Jack Rudy, and Bradley's all offer syrups to stock up the bar.

BITTERS

With only a dash or two, aromatic bitters have the ability to brighten or darken, invigorate or mellow, a sophisticated cocktail. So what is bitters? Bitters is a potent combination of high grain alcohol infused with a blend of roots and flowers, fruit peels and tree bark, herbs, spices, and other botanicals. Many might assume that bitterness is not a desired quality in a beverage, but the truth is that bitters does not necessarily make your cocktail bitter. It can be a great aid in taming a sweet cocktail, it keeps the palate fresh between sips, and it imparts botanical and citrus essences. Bitterness, in proportion, delivers a refined component to a cocktail's palate.

Artisanal production of diverse goods has been budding in communities all over the Earth, and one prime example is the bitters market. Within the past decade a multitude of small-batch bitters has begun lining bars in rapid succession, basking, once again, in popular mixology. From recreating a pre-Prohibition classic to inventing a brand new cocktail, bitters is a significant component. Many bars now tote house-made bitters, and an ever-increasing number of craft productions are coming to market.

Bitters is not a new cocktail ingredient, however; it has just been neglected for some time. Until recently, that is. The most well-known and oldest of all surviving bitters, Angostura, was created by German doctor Johann Gottlieb Benjamin Siegert in approximately 1824. The name comes from the town of Angostura (now Ciudad Bolivar), Venezuela, where he moved in 1820. The recipe remains a vaulted secret, known only to five minds.

House-made bitters from the Columbia Room.

The first flourish bitters experienced was in early nineteenth-century London and America. Many brands originated as medicinal preparations claiming unproven benefits, just like tonic, but came to be appreciated as a flavoring agent for adventurous nineteenth-century mixologists. It became so essential that a drink would not be defined as a cocktail without bitters' inclusion. Before the term grew to encapsulate any mixed alcoholic beverage, a cocktail was a mixture of any spirit base, water, sugar, and bitters.

The medicinal aspect of bitters was put under scrutiny as America passed the Pure Food and Drug Act of 1906, requiring producers to remove words like "cure" from the label, limit alcohol content, and provide the ingredients. This, in combination with the 1919 Volstead Act and ensuing period of Prohibition, caused bitters to lose appeal and footing. During Prohibition the quality of most illicit liquor was so poor that people turned to potent juices and syrups as mixers to mask the subpar taste, and most bitters producers could no longer legally sell their product. These blows reduced the number of makers down to a few and effectively abolished bitters into the shadows for a time.

ORGANIC

FARMER'S™

BOTANICAL

SMALL BATCH ORGANIC

GIN

Organic Gin handcrafted for ultimate smoothness
from Juniper, Elderflower, Lemon Grass, Coriander,
Angelica Root & other Select Botanicals

USDA
ORGANIC

750ML • 46.7% ALC/VOL • (93.4 PROOF)

Gin & Bitters
Gin Pahit (or Pink Gin Cocktail)

To truly appreciate the current cocktail revival, it is good to look back. After all, modern cocktails are the direct descendants of their historical predecessors, and every mixologist's palate should be developed through classics. As bartenders travel and share recipes, and consumers look for exotic cocktails, many variations ensue, hence three different names for the same tipple. The following recipe is taken directly from *The Gentleman's Companion Volume II*.

Ingredients Needed:

London dry or Old Tom gin
Angostura bitters

"Take a thin, stemmed cocktail glass. Shake in 4 or 5 dashes of Angostura, tip the glass like the tower of Pisa and twirl it between thumb and fingers. Whatever Angostura sticks to the glass through capillary attraction is precisely the right amount. . . . Gently pour off the extra bitters that do not cling. Fill the glass with gin. That's all. . . . We personally drop a chip of ice into our Gin Pahit glass; or also twist a curl of lime or lemon peel atop, for its aromatics. One of the world's greatest, simplest drinks."

With bitters' recent reclaimed fame, producers are pushing the bounds and trying new concepts. Bittermens (New Orleans) produces a healthy line of bitters including unusual suspects such as Xocolatl Mole, Peppercake Gingerbread, and Squire Nut Pecan Vanilla bitters. Innovations like these are fueling bartenders across the globe to step up and craft new and interesting cocktails. The Bitter Truth (Germany) line of bitters has been expanding its offerings since opening in 2006. Included in their product line are bottles of orange, celery, grapefruit, lemon, and Old Time Aromatic. They also offer a variation dubbed Jerry Thomas' Bitters, a nod to the nineteenth-century American bartender and author. Other brands to sample are Regans', Peychauds, and Dr. Adam Elmegirab's.

A great online resource for purchasing unique bitters is www.cocktailkingdom.com.

VERMOUTH

(This article on vermouth is provided by Ben Koenig, manager at Discovery Wines, New York City.)

In this innovative era of cocktails, great care is being paid to all facets of the cocktail-making process. Whether the topic is artisanal bitters, house-cured pickles, or specialty ice trays, every ingredient matters and plays its role in a well-crafted drink. Vermouth is part of this process and deserves a place in any well-stocked liquor cabinet (keep it in the fridge after opening). Luckily for us, vermouth has garnered significant attention in the last few years from producers and enthusiasts, and many wonderful examples are now available on the US market.

So, what is vermouth? Essentially, it is a fortified wine that has been doctored with an array of botanicals, herbs, and spices. An innocuous white wine serves as the base, neutral grape spirit contributes extra alcohol, and then various flavorings are added to give vermouth its particular character. These can include but are not limited to citrus peel, cinnamon, cloves, quinine, cardamom, marjoram, chamomile, coriander, juniper, hyssop, and ginger. For those who think this concoction sounds tonic—associating its sweet, but bitter flavors with medicine—there is a well-founded reason why. Throughout previous centuries in Europe, China, and India, these wines were made to combat stomachaches, intestinal parasites, and other maladies for which antibiotics did not exist. By the end of the nineteenth century, however, vermouth was becoming an integral part of the cocktail craze, and that tradition carries on today.

Ostensibly, there are two kinds of vermouth: sweet (which can be either red or white) and dry (which is almost invariably white). One can enjoy their singular complexities neat or on the rocks, but vermouth has become most popular in its application to cocktails. Every vermouth boasts a unique blend of herbs, botanicals, and spices that enhances certain spirits. For this reason, vermouth as a whole lends itself to improvisation and play.

Take for example the classic manhattan cocktail, in which rye whiskey or bourbon is combined with Angostura bitters and sweet vermouth to create

Classic Bronx Cocktail

1 oz. dry gin
1 oz. Italian sweet vermouth
1 oz. French dry vermouth
1 oz. fresh orange juice
Orange peel garnish (optional)

Combine all ingredients over ice in a mixer. Shake and strain into a frozen cocktail glass. May garnish with an orange peel.

a richly flavored, autumnal cocktail. Different vermouths offer different flavors and bring out a spectrum of secondary characteristics in the whiskey. Dolin's Red Vermouth is drier and more elegant than Punt e Mes' Carpano Antica and, therefore, calls for a leaner whiskey with spicier, rye-based flavors. Alternatively, Carpano Anitca is a decadently sweet vermouth that plays well with brawnier bourbons.

A more apt example for a book about gin is the perfect martini, also known as the 50-50. In this rendition of the ubiquitous martini, dry vermouth and gin are combined in equal portions and garnished with an olive or lemon peel. Such a simple cocktail relies on the quality and distinction of its ingredients and presents the perfect opportunity to highlight delicious vermouth. The spry, citrusy flavors of Vya Extra Dry Vermouth, produced in the San Joaquin Valley of California, are hard to dislike and pair well with a variety of London dry gins. Classic examples of dry vermouth such as Noilly Prat, Cinzano, and Dolin are softer, more floral, and better suited to the wildly aromatic American gins.

America's rejuvenated love for cocktails has resulted in a vibrant community of domestic winemakers trying their hands at vermouth, continually experimenting and tweaking their recipes in the hopes of creating a uniquely delicious product. Producers such as Imbue in Oregon, Atsby in New York, and Vya in California are crafting distinctive aromatized wines that redefine the boundaries of traditional vermouth. For example, Imbue's Rose Petal & Thorn is made in the style of an Italian amaro, offering a richer texture and intensely bitter finish. Atsby adds unfamiliar botanicals, such as Chinese anise and holy basil, to contribute exotic aromas and flavors. While domestic vermouths represent a tiny percentage of worldwide production, there is an unprecedented variety of sensational American vermouths to be had.

IMBUE CELLARS

IMBUE CELLARS
PATTON VALLEY VINEYARDS, GASTON, OREGON
WWW.IMBUECELLARS.COM

IMBUE LABELS:

Bittersweet Vermouth
Petal & Thorn Aperitif Wine

G in is only half the equation that makes a classic martini. Vermouth is the other crucial ingredient, and it is finally starting to get its due thanks to the craft movement. Many craft vermouths are great for sipping straight, as well. I recently had the pleasure to sit down with Neil Kopplin, co-owner and national sales executive of Imbue Cellars, to discuss his views on all things vermouth.

"It isn't a martini without vermouth; it's just gin or vodka," Kopplin explains. "A martini is a cocktail; it's not a word that should be tossed around just because your drink is served up. This topic makes me a touch surly because I've got definite opinions about it. A martini is three parts gin, one part vermouth, with orange bitters and a twist. Yes, olives are a nice touch, too, because a true martini has the slightest touch of sweetness balanced with some salty olives; it can be heavenly. Each home bartender and drinker should experiment with different gins, vermouths, proportions, and garnishes to decide what they like best."

> "It isn't a martini without vermouth; it's just gin or vodka."

In my discussions with American and British vermouth producers, it became clear that there exists a divide between the continents. So I ask Kopplin to explain the differences.

"European producers have rules about what has to be in vermouth. American producers don't have the same exact stipulations. Most American producers have chosen to use great wine as a base to the product, which leaves it a lot more drinkable for the Americanized palate. We can also push the boundaries of styles of vermouth. It leaves a lot more room for creativity.

"I think that American producers are finally starting to catch the eye of European producers. European producers are very protective of their traditions, as they should be. However, we don't have those traditions. Europe provides us with inspiration, and we create our own style around that. We don't have an aperitif-drinking culture here. So even though the inspiration of what we do as American producers is inspired by the Europeans, the earth provides us with different bounties to draw from. Plus, we have a much different audience to appease."

I ask, finally, what reactions he has experienced from Europeans sampling his vermouths.

"A lot of European producers have a difficult time recognizing our vermouth as vermouth, simply because it doesn't contain the namesake of vermouth: wormwood. Wormwood is regulated by the FDA [Food and Drug Administration] and TTB [Alcohol and Tobacco Tax and Trade Bureau] because of laws on the books that date back to making absinthe illegal. Not all start-up vermouth producers can afford to use their entire budgets on pushing their product through TTB thujone testing, so most choose to leave it out. That one omission sparks passions on both sides."

Humphrey Bogart sips gin in The African Queen.

BAR CONGRESS

200 CONGRESS AVE.
AUSTIN, TEXAS
WWW.CONGRESSAUSTIN.COM

Step out into the Texas sun, jump in the rental car and I'm on my way to meet Jason Stevens, bar manager at Austin's revered Bar Congress. The cocktail and wine bar features a very sleek and refined lounge décor. In contrast to some other venues that create their atmosphere with randomly placed mismatched furniture, Bar Congress' uniform style works for it. A ruler-straight row of leather stools, bellied up to the bar, await the evening's thirsty crowd. Opposite the bar, cushioned seating lines the wall under repeated decorative chandlers and large windows. The space feels very open. Bar Congress offers a "strong commitment to classically executed craft cocktails" and boasts that patrons will see no high fructose corn syrup or other artificial sweeteners on the premises. Many of their mixers are house-made, providing truly one-of-a-kind libations. Private party rooms and a restaurant, Second, are all linked to the bar from the interior.

> "The flavor profiles of gin are fairly well established, allowing creativity within the range of tradition."

I approach and introduce myself to Stevens, a talented and friendly bartender with a passion for creating fresh craft cocktails. The first thing that catches my eye is a bottle system behind the bar. Stevens tells me, "These are our shift shots." "Shift shots?" I repeat. He kindly explains, "Shift shots are a simple combination of either a base sprit or aperitif liqueur with amaro and possibly a dash of bitters. They are undiluted, unchilled, and typically served up. We keep eight different shift shots on an enomatic wine-tap system. I feature known and loved combinations such as the 50-50 (half Fernet and half Campari, also known as a 'Ferrari') along with house combinations like the wooden ships (Cynar, Rhum agricole, Mole bitters, and saline) or the good morning, good night (Rittenhouse rye, Nardini amaro, and a dash of espresso)."

On the menu I see they also offer a shift-shot variation made with genever, called Dutch Courage.

I know Bar Congress prides itself on having each style of gin represented on their shelves, so I ask about how that plays into the distinct experience their patrons receive. Stevens explains, "At Bar Congress, I feel it's important to offer the guest an opportunity to learn more about the sprits they love. Although our selection isn't expansive, I make sure to carry many styles of gin beyond London dry style. Old Tom, various styles of genever, and New World botanicals are all featured heavily on our cocktail menu, and the response to these lesser-known styles of gins from our guests has been overwhelmingly positive."

Next I ask Stevens about the house-made mixers. He says, "Most of the non-spritous ingredients in our cocktails are made by hand in house. I use local and organic products whenever possible. I avoid using modified sugars as much as possible, focusing on raw, natural sweeteners." It certainly seems to attract a cocktail-savvy crowd. After speaking about the importance of using fresh and local sources I am curious what botanicals are indigenous to the Austin region. Stevens says, "Rosemary grows like weeds here in Texas and has found its way into several local gins, most notably Waterloo gin. We also see local lavender and Rio Star grapefruit (from south Texas) appearing more and more in Texas-bred spirits."

Agent Ribbons

Dry, crisp, lightly tart, with subtle earthiness.

1½ oz. Ford's gin (for local gin, I use Genius gin)
½ oz. Dolin dry vermouth
¼ oz. honey syrup
¾ oz. Rio Star grapefruit juice
½ oz. fresh lemon juice
1 tbsp. Marolo chamomile grappa
1 slice grapefruit peel

Combine all in a shaker over ice and shake. Fine strain into a chilled coupe and garnish with a grapefruit peel.

WATERLOO

Hand-Crafted

TEXAS-STYLE

GIN

Distilled from grain in Austin, Texas

750 ML 47% Alc./Vol.(94° Proof)

"When did you begin to notice that gin was capturing the eye of the craft distillery movement in Austin?" I ask. "I've noticed local distillers' interest in gin growing over the past few years, and the number of new local gins on the market grow quickly during that time. From a new distiller's perspective, I imagine gin being a good first step into the world of making boutique spirits. The flavor profiles of gin are fairly well established, allowing creativity within the range of tradition. Gin's usual base, neutral grain spirit, doesn't need to be produced by the distiller, allowing space and resources to be focused on the flavor of the gin itself," Stevens says. I thank Jason for his hospitality, knowledge and time, and hit the road.

San Martin

An amazing classic Martinez variation; drinks like a botanical manhattan.

1½ oz. St. George Terroir gin
1½ oz. Cocchi di Torino vermouth
¼ oz. Green Chartreuse

Combine all in a glass filled with cubed ice and stir. Strain into a chilled Nick and Nora or coupe glass. Leave ungarnished.

A DROP OF H$_2$O

Seasoned whiskey and scotch drinkers have known this for years: a drop of water does not dilute the tipple but rather enlivens its core essence. This is not just true of whiskey and brown liquors. The chemistry behind the benefits of adding a drop or two of water is as follows. The aroma, or the nose, of a spirit clings tightly to the alcohol, but as water is introduced, diluting the liquid, aroma molecules are loosened from their source and evaporate into the air with the water. Put some gin in a glass and smell. Then add a few drops of water, swirl, and smell again. The botanicals should be wafting up to your nose in a more prominent manner (gins with higher alcohol content will be most affected by water). The sense of smell is just as important as taste when eating or drinking. Give this a try in your next strong gin cocktail or gin on the rocks.

A PHILADELPHIA
GIN TASTING

EVENT HELD AT 6 P.M. ON OCTOBER 29, 2013
SINE STUDIOS
127 SOUTH 22ND STREET
PHILADELPHIA, PENNSYLVANIA

Throughout my travels and research, I ended up accumulating a lot of gin. A *lot* of gin. Gins that many of my friends in Philadelphia had never seen before. More gin than I could drink alone. And so in an effort to garner a multitude of both expert and consumer opinions, I put together the following team for a gin tasting:

Katie Loeb. Mixologist, author, beverage consultant to a multitude of cocktail-savvy venues, and one of the first proponents of Philadelphia's craft-cocktail scene.

Sarah Lockwood. Bartender at the American Sardine Bar in Philadelphia, and cocktail enthusiast.

Dynamic duo Sarah Bonkowski and James Hearne. Sarah is a food-service lifer and was invaluable to me during my search for exquisite venues. James, also known in Philadelphia as the hardest-working man in show business, is a friend, talented singer-songwriter, and gin appreciator.

Mike Lawson. Stellar photographer who I enlisted in capturing the evening in photographs. We've known each other since the sixth grade and have sipped many martinis and G&Ts together over the years.

Katie Barbato. My wife, who I am slowly and subliminally converting into a gin drinker, is a singer-songwriter who can silence a room with her voice.

Taylor Kogut. An engineer at Sine Studios who enjoys adult beverages and is always up for new experiences.

Philadelphia may be the world's largest small town. Although none of the invitees, myself included, realized it prior, everyone either knew each other from previous encounters or were connected through friends and venues.

Now let's slip into the present tense and have some fun.

First we set up our game plan. We place barrel-aged to one side, sloe gin and liqueurs on the other, London and American dries and variations in the middle, a few bottles of Old Tom grouped together, and some more peculiar specimens in the corner. Beautifully unique and glimmering gin bottles are now spread across the table before us, surrounded by place settings marked with rocks glasses. To the side we place a bucket of ice, a container to discard unwanted samples, and a rinsing bucket. A charcuterie from the famous Philadelphia staple, Di Bruno Brothers, sits to the side, ready to provide enough stamina to sample a significant number of gins and to reset our palates between sips. We decide to save the heavier barrel-aged and liqueur varieties for last, since we assume they will be heaviest on the taste buds. We joke about how many of these we'll be able to get through before it turns ugly.

As we gather around the table I ask Loeb a question I had been asking often in my interviews. "Are you a bartender or a mixologist?" Katie says, "While some of my cohorts are deeply offended by the mixologist title,

I have no such bad reaction to it. I figure I'm both. Bartender when I'm literally tending customers at the bar. Mixologist when I'm doing recipe development."

We decide we will sip each gin at room temperature, followed by a sip stirred with an ice cube to see how chilling the liquid affects it.

And we're off!

We start with the frosted bottle of Jensen Old Tom. Even before sipping, the gin's nose provides a sweet citrus smell. At room temperature this gin has a little pepper on the tail, but is pleasant. After a sip, we each drop in an ice cube and cool it down. This cooling really livens up the gin. Lockwood surmises, "I guess the reason the viscosity changed so much with only one ice cube is because this is an Old Tom and the sugar content is higher." Loeb responds, "Yes, I'm sure if we had this in a wine glass at room temperature and swirled it you would probably see legs, and with an ice cube it would sheet off really quickly." (Note: *legs* is a term, also used in the wine industry, to describe the residue that will hang on the sides of the glass in a syrupy fashion after a swirl, signifying higher alcohol content.) We sample Jensen's London dry as well and, as a group, rate it as a quality gin. Maybe good for a cilantro gimlet, without any cilantro, someone suggests with tongue in cheek. We rinse our glasses.

We try Ransom Old Tom, and a few at the table who had previously tried it agree that it is their favorite gin for the Martinez cocktail. Then Lockwood reaches for the Russell Henry Malaysian lime gin. We joke about distilleries trying to outdo each other by procuring more and more abstract ingredients. Loeb adds, "You know the unicorn tears thing—it's not that hard to catch them, but it *is* really hard to make them cry!" I see interest building as my neighbors smell the juice's aroma wafting up from their glasses. The lime essence pronounces itself in a subtle, smooth manner. We all sip. Silence, for a moment, and then the room breaks out in reaction.

Bonkowski: "A bucket of flowers! That tastes wonderful."

Lockwood: "How light, how unexpectedly light."

Loeb: "That tastes more like St. Germain and gin! That is really light. That's 47.07 percent? That doesn't taste hot at all!"

Barbato: "Wow, *gin*!"

Rinse and repeat.

(clockwise from bottom left): Taylor Kogut,
Matt Teacher, Katie Barbato, James Hearne,
Sarah Bonkowski, Katie Loeb, Sarah Lockwood.)

We tried many more excellent and interesting gins—Barr Hill made from their farmed honey, Monkey 47, Big Gin Bourbon-Barreled, Wire Works Special Reserve, Waterloo Barrel-Aged, Corsair Barrel-Aged, and coming to a close with Greenhook Ginsmiths Beach Plum Gin Liqueur, a seasonal specialty. As we wrap up we leave some bottles unopened, for another time. We all say our thank-yous and good-byes. Loeb shares the news that after the tasting, upon arriving home she will be drinking a nonalcoholic rehydrating cocktail she had come up with. She has graciously shared it on the following page.

A Cautionary Tale:
A Preventative Rehydration Beverage

16 oz. unflavored coconut water
3–4 oz. orange or pineapple juice
1/8 tsp. salt

Stir together and drink before bed to avoid hangover.

HOME GIN TASTING

Materials Needed:
Lots of different gins, glassware (rocks glasses work well), ice cubes
in a bucket with serving tongs, a dump bucket to discard unwanted
samples, a rinsing receptacle to clean glasses between tastings,
notecards, pens, and friends.

Suggestions:
• Try first tasting each gin straight, at room temperature, followed by
a sip chilled by adding an ice cube and stirring. Note how the gins'
viscosity changes when cooled.

• Try a tasting comparing all gins from a specific category, such as
all London drys, all new Americans, or all aged gins.

• Bring together a group of tasters with different palates and see if
opinions differ. Hand out notecards and pens and have everyone log
their initial reactions before discussion.

AUXILIARY
SOLIDS

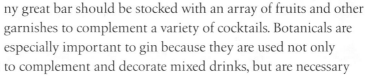 ny great bar should be stocked with an array of fruits and other garnishes to complement a variety of cocktails. Botanicals are especially important to gin because they are used not only to complement and decorate mixed drinks, but are necessary in the production of gin. In addition to the chief flavoring agent, juniper berries, gin is created by macerating and/or distilling a collection of aromatics found all over the globe.

Botanicals

The term *botanical* (n.) encompasses a dictionary-length catalog of plant life. The *Merriam-Webster Dictionary* defines it as, "of or relating to plants or botany." In the work of art that is gin, botanicals are the paint, the still is the brush, and the distiller is the painter. Neutral spirit, which vodka is considered by some to be, is the canvas. When a craft distillery prepares to launch a new gin label, or any label for that matter, a lot of time, research, and experimentation must precede. In addition to choosing the still and

distillation procedure, the perfect blend of botanicals must be gathered and assembled. Distilling is an art. A gin's flavor profile represents its author's voice and opinion as to what their region's gin should be, and announces it for public verdict. Some distilleries claim their water source as a key, while others claim their still—both of which are important—but in the end, if quality botanicals are not used, it all may be in vain.

A distiller's choice as to the grouping of botanicals used to flavor their gin is a major factor in how it will most be enjoyed. Initially many gins were produced with limited local botanicals, depending on the region. As the spice trade developed, more and more unique herbs and spices ventured out across the Earth. Today, with our streamlined distribution channels it has never been easier for distillers to collect their resources from around the world. Labels now have the ability to use interesting imports and local produce, such as the Russell Henry Malaysian lime gin or Letherbee's prairie grass gin.

Using local, fresh, and organic botanicals when possible, as well as a stellar base spirit and water supply, is a conviction many hold within the gin community. As gin production spreads over continents, sprawling to all corners of the Earth, the opportunity for new distillers to develop gin labels featuring exotic plant life has arrived. Greenhook Ginsmiths in Brooklyn, New York, utilize the East Coast's beach plums for their liqueur. Vermont-based Caledonia Spirits uses its freshly farmed honey in its Barr Hill gin. In addition to distillers discovering local botanicals, the sourcing of ingredients from remote locations has become a lot easier as well. In addition to the Malaysian limes, Russell Henry in Northern California sources Hawaiian white ginger for another label. We should expect to see even more exotic gins arriving shortly and regularly.

CROSS SECTION ON BOTANICALS

The world is a bounty of botanicals, and much of that bounty is now being utilized to infuse incredible flavor profiles in gins. Here are just a few of the most classic and innovative selections made by discerning distillers.

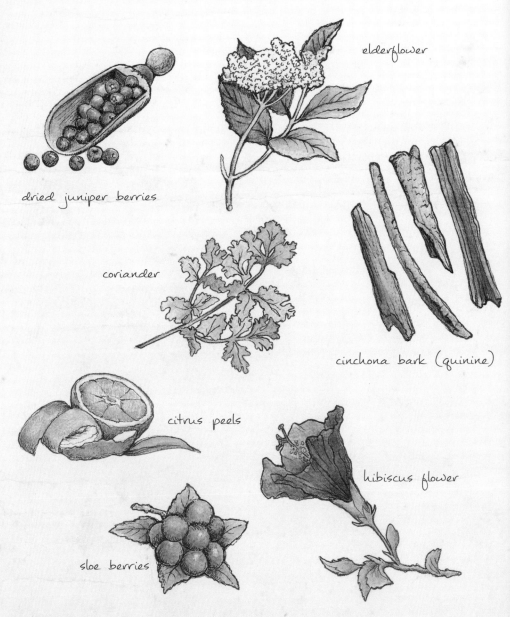

elderflower

dried juniper berries

coriander

cinchona bark (quinine)

citrus peels

hibiscus flower

sloe berries

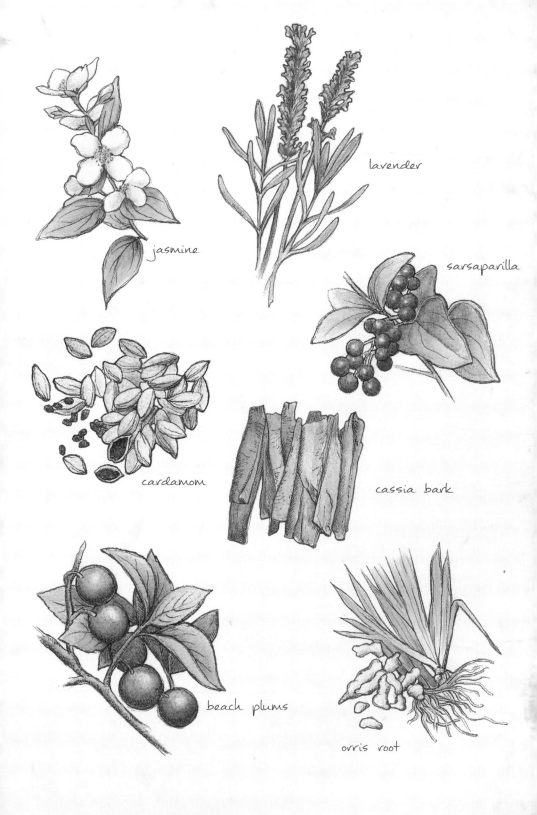

jasmine

lavender

sarsaparilla

cardamom

cassia bark

beach plums

orris root

Booth's ad from the 1930s.

LEMONS UP WITH A TWIST

(This article on lemons is provided by Janet Bukovinsky Teacher, cookbook publisher and author, New Hope, Pennsylvania.)

Lemon's role in a gin martini is indisputable. No other garnish is as clean, bright, acidic, and coolly neutral.

"A large thin slice of lemon peel" was James Bond's directive to a French bartender in *Casino Royale*, circa 1953. That shiny yellow lozenge of fruit skin, or zest, was called for to quick-infuse a three-to-one gin-to-vodka mixture called the vesper, to impart a citric slap that elevated it from a mere boozehound's sop to something bold, elegant and very masculine. Lemon has a way of doing that—enhancing whatever it touches by seeming to shake it awake.

The most commonly encountered varieties of lemon are the Eureka, with a textured skin, and the Lisbon, which is smoother and has fewer seeds. Probably native to Asia, they're grown in Florida, California, and the Mediterranean area on evergreen trees that range from 10- to 20-feet tall. The best lemons are small and heavy for their size, with shiny, pliant skin that is taut but not rock-hard, which indicates dryness. They may look nice piled in a bowl on top of your bar, but lemons should be stored in a plastic bag in the refrigerator, where they'll stay fresh for a couple of weeks. At room temperature, they'll get soft and moldy before the week is up.

When using lemons in a cocktail, take the time to first scrub the fruit under warm water with a textured dish sponge, to remove wax and dirt. Its peel is the lemon's packaging, and you don't want to know what kind of places it was rolling around in on its journey from the tree to your bar. In addition, conventionally grown lemons are waxed to prolong shelf life and freshness. Thus the peel may be coated with products containing ethanol, ethyl alcohol, petroleum, soaps, and other synthetic substances. Whenever possible, choose organic lemons, which are grown without pesticides and chemical fertilizers; if wax is used, it will be plant-based. Chances are you'll notice the difference, for a farm-to-table fresh sliver of lemon peel really distinguishes a gin cocktail.

For culinary use, many chefs prefer the Meyer lemon, native to California, which has a thinner skin than the Eureka or Lisbon. In a cocktail, however, the Meyer's complex floral aroma—the reason it's so revered these days in the food world—can interfere with gin's own flavor profile. Nothing tanks a crisp, dry martini like a noseful of flowery Meyer lemon perfume.

Strictly speaking, in a gin drink you want only the lemon's shiny yellow peel, pared sharply away from the dull white pith, which can be bitter and lacks the zest's pointed flavor. An all-purpose vegetable peeler works well, as long as it's fairly new and its blade is sharp. A kitchen tool made specifically for lemon zesting is also effective, but be sure to use the larger-hooked end meant for creating a robust single strip of peel rather than the multi-hooked part, which yields a little haystack of thin peels meant for decorating cakes or infusing risotto. A good half-inch slice is necessary for eliciting a spurt of fragrant lemon oil when it's twisted over the martini glass, then dropped in for effect.

There's no secret to making that classic, decorative cocktail garnish—the twirly spiral of lemon peel—except a steady hand, a sharp device, and a little bit of confidence. Holding the lemon vertically in one hand and wielding the tool of your choice in the other—a simple, sharp paring knife works very well—begin near the top of the lemon and exert just enough force to scrape up all of the yellow zest but not enough to grab the white pith below. Cutting spherically while turning the lemon will make a spiral, while cutting from top to bottom can produce a straight one- to two-inch strip. Depending on skill, a single lemon should produce between four and eight twists. Chances are, the long tendril of peel will break before you reach the other end of the lemon, but once it's been rubbed on the rim of the glass, draped artfully over the edge, or is safely afloat within the icy drink, who cares? Suddenly, the room smells happy and fresh, like lemonade, and it's time to relish the first, best sip of that cocktail. No wonder they call it zest.

Gin and tonic with
lemon and ice.

Vintage ad from 1937.

BROKEN SHAKER

2727 INDIAN CREEK DRIVE
MIAMI BEACH, FLORIDA
WWW.THEFREEHAND.COM/VENUES/THE-BROKEN-SHAKER

South Beach, Miami, is a world unto its own. Its increasingly sophisticated cocktail culture has pushed aside the cheap drinks in plastic cups that used to be its hallmark. This sea change has been driven by a younger generation of cocktail visionaries such as Elad Zvi and Gabriel Orta. Upon arriving in Miami in 2009, the two started Bar Lab (www.bar-lab.com), a cocktail-program customization service for bars and venues. Then, in search of their own spot, the pair started a temporary pop-up bar at the new Freehand Hotel, an affordable hostel-style hotel, named Broken Shaker. The comfortable yet hip hostel atmosphere lent itself incredibly well to the bar Zvi and Orta launched. It came as no surprise that, after its closing, patrons of the cocktail scene they had established were saddened to discover its absence. So Zvi and Orta struck a deal to make Broken Shaker a permanent fixture.

I'm happy to be traveling with a crew on this particular adventure, including my wife, Katie; an old high school friend; and Florida bartender Keanan

Elad Zvi and Gabriel Orta.

McCabe and his girlfriend CarrieLee Anderson. After we arrive by taxi in front of the three-story building, we stroll into the hostel's lobby, a big open space that feels down to earth but not uncared for.

We move through the lobby to the outdoor backyard where the Broken Shaker resides. Strands of lights are strewn across the night sky. Hammocks, scattered trees, and clusters of tables, chairs and couches sit under umbrellas creating an enjoyable Floridian atmosphere. A pool stretches away from the hostel.

As we are seated at our table, we begin to peruse the menu. I order the garden martini featuring a blend of fresh celery and allspice cordial, Noilly Prat Ambré, and Bombay dry gin. This cocktail's name reflects its taste, a delicious fresh spin on a martini. As we sip our cocktails and a charcuterie arrives, Elad approaches the table to greet us. He is holding a bottle of jenever, the Dutch predecessor to gin, that we had spoken about on the phone prior to meeting. This bottle was a gift to Elad and is not currently a featured ingredient in any Broken Shaker cocktails. The label, Rutte & ZN Oude Simon, is one I have never seen before. He kindly pours us each a taste at room temperature. It is definitely unique from the typical London dry varieties, and its nutty and herbaceous personality would lend itself to some interesting libations.

We chat about the great vibe they have cultivated, and Elad tells me, "We are all about fun, serving the guests and not our ego. We don't have a door guy and there are no reservations." You can tell. In a town where trivial aesthetic is often the norm, the guests here are relaxed, friendly, and having fun. They also offer a daily punch, which serves four to eight and contains the guest's choice of base spirit mixed with fruit and botanicals. It's too late in the evening for us to travel down that path, but we agree to return someday to sample this tempting punch. I thank Elad for his time, drink, and hospitality, and we hop in a cab back to the Delano Hotel.

Garden Martini

2 oz. Bombay dry gin
1 oz. Noilly Prat Ambre
¾ oz. celery and allspice cordial
Orange twist

Pour ingredients into a mixing glass with ice cubes. Stir well. Strain into a chilled cocktail glass. Garnish with an orange twist.

Pistachio Gin Fizz

2 oz. Bombay dry gin infused with pistachios
1 oz. Lillet Blanc
¾ oz. lemon juice
1 egg white (optional)
Lemon twist
Mint leaf

Pour ingredients into a cocktail shaker filled with ice. Shake vigorously (extra vigorously if using the egg white to ensure it mixes thoroughly). Strain into a chilled highball glass with ice cubes. Garnish with a lemon twist and mint.

OLIVES

(This article on olives is provided by Janet Bukovinsky Teacher.)

What did the bartender say to Charles Dickens? "What'll it be, buddy— olive or twist?"

"Diver in the depths of a martini," as the great food writer Waverly Root described the humble olive, it is perhaps civilization's most ancient fruit. Like grapes, their botanical compatriot, olives have provided sustenance both cultural and physical throughout recorded history. The olive branch, with its silvery gray leaves, is a classic symbol of peace, while a round olive in a conical martini glass is an iconic image that bespeaks the good life as much as a comet of bubbles in a champagne flute.

Olives give the martini drinker a reason to drain her glass, a juicy, flavorsome reward that contrasts brilliantly with gin's acerbic character. They're sustenance in the form of a cured Mediterranean tree fruit. But which olive goes best with an icy gin martini?

The classic martini garnish is the generic green Spanish olive, often stuffed for taste and textural contrast with a morsel of roasted red pepper.

There are many brands of gourmet-quality brine-cured "martini olives" on the market. The better brands are olives called Queen. Look for jars of large imported olives stuffed with a meaty piece of pimiento pepper in a well-salted brine. (A quick splash of that brine, of course, is key to the creation of a dirty martini.) In the case of bottled martini olives, you definitely get what you pay for: the bigger the olive, the higher, in general, the price tag. Which is not to dismiss the traditional small stuffed green olive, those grape-sized ones that tend to get threaded onto a cocktail skewer in threes—there's no discounting their singular retro appeal. True devotees may find that martini olives packed in vermouth, offered by several companies, are the ultimate convenience and the fruit of all their cocktail dreams. A dash of that vermouth marinade makes a singular-tasting martini.

Meanwhile, drinkers interested in true culinary excellence may want to look beyond the jars to the olive-bar selection at their nearest upscale supermarket. These green olives are inevitably coated in olive oil, which leaves a slick upon the surface of a pristine gin martini. The thing to do is to take them home, drain and transfer to a jar, then add vermouth to cover. That extra effort is well worth it to enjoy the tasty varieties of imported olives just begging to be tossed into a martini. The downside is that many of these fruits contain pits, about which hungry cocktail companions should be warned.

"Castelvetrano is a superb martini olive," says Emilio Companioni, a Philadelphia-area specialty-foods expert. "They have a clean, bright flavor that complements gin, and since they are available already pitted, you can use them as is or stuff them with blue cheese, jalapeno, citrus, almonds or garlic for a dirty martini." Grown in Sicily, the plump, substantial Castelvetrano provides a serious mouthful for the gin drinker who's ready to savor the pleasure of the contrasting flavors. Just as big but milder and sweeter of flesh are the Italian Cerignola olives. They're a brighter green in color than Castelvetrano. A tasty alternative is the crisp little Picholine, a Moroccan olive that's often available pitted. Arbequina, a small olive from the Catalonia region of Spain, delivers a mild, savory taste but has a substantial pit. Lucques is another gourmet-quality green variety to keep an eye out for.

A classic set of bar tools should include cocktail picks for impaling unpitted or stuffed olives. Often sold in sets of six, the picks are available in materials from bamboo to stainless steel to heirloom-quality sterling silver. When serving a martini with unpitted olives, it's nice to provide a little saucer or dish for the discarded pits, but they can also be discreetly deposited in a paper cocktail napkin. It's a rare martini drinker who leaves his uneaten olives in the glass.

ICE VARIATIONS

There are four core varieties of ice that bars and mixologists have at their disposal today—cubed ice, block ice, shaved ice, and cracked ice. There are also other variations such as the ice sphere, more often used for whiskey drinks. It is commonly agreed that most cocktails are more enjoyable when cold and not at room temperature. Ice, historically, was the way to chill a cocktail—even if the drink was not served over ice, it was still employed during shaking or stirring. In fiercely shaken cocktails, such as a martini, ice can even change the texture by creating small ice chips that sneak through the strainer into the serving glass. Today, many, such as Alessandro Palazzi at Dukes Bar in London, negate ice altogether for many cocktails, choosing to keep glassware and gin bottles in the freezer.

With any form of ice, a central belief among aficionados is that you have to start with filtered or distilled water. Starting with water that has an "odor" or a "taste" to it will most certainly impart its tainted essence into your drink as it melts.

When deciding which form of ice to use, the drink itself must first be considered.

CUBES

Ice cubes are great for use in a stirred cocktail, a drink on the rocks, or fused together in totem-pole fashion and stood up in a Collins glass. Cubes melt at a somewhat slow rate, although not as slow as a sphere, which affords little dilution provided the drink is consumed in a somewhat timely fashion. A bartender may also use a Lewis bag and mallet to turn cubes into crushed ice for use in cocktails such as a gin fizz.

Block Ice

Block ice is considered by many, myself included, to be the most unadulterated ice. In the past, most ice began as blocks and it was up to bartenders to divide it as they saw fit. Today, block ice is usually created in what looks like a horizontal freezer where water is circulated through the tank repeatedly as it slowly cools. The result is some of the purest and clearest ice available. This gives the bartender the opportunity to break up the ice as needed for specific cocktails.

Shaved Ice

Although it's not often seen in gin drinks, for the adventurous, shaved ice is the choice if you're looking to create an alcoholic snow cone, slurry, or slushy.

COLD GIN

Gin should almost always be consumed as cold as possible.

Gin is a malleable presence, bound not only by the capability of its creator but by the savvy of its consumer. Why should you keep a bottle of gin in the freezer? Because it not only changes the texture in a beneficial way for cocktails such as a martini, but it replaces the need to shake vigorously with a more consistent and steady swift stir, and makes for a more consistent tipple. If the whole vermouth/gin blend is pre-prepared, such as they do at Harry's Bar in Venice, Italy, it negates the need for ice entirely and is pulled from the freezer already with the desired viscosity.

CRACKED ICE

Cracked ice has a much smaller surface area and is suited for use in frozen drinks such as a frozen gin fizz. Blenders are not all that consistent, and using smaller pieces of ice ensures a dependable result.

GARNISHES

Any well-stocked bar looking to provide ample cocktail variations should include a selection of fresh garnishes for their cocktails. The best garnishes are always procured to order—lemon zest is peeled as the drink is ordered, olives are stored in brine, and mint and other leaves are stored in ice water. Other popular garnishes include maraschino cherries, limes, oranges, cucumber, celery stalks, onions, apple slices, and a variety of berries. Fruits and some vegetables may be cut into thinly sliced wheels, thick wedges and other varieties of artistic shapes depending on the cocktail application and

desired presentation. It is also in fashion to toast certain garnishes, such as an orange or lemon peel, in pursuit of a more developed flavor. While perhaps not considered garnishes, egg whites, grated nutmeg, salt and pepper, and fresh cream are also used in many cocktails. It's a lot to ask of a home bartender, but knowing what to look out for when checking out a new venue is always helpful.

BARTENDER'S TOOLKIT

As with any trade, you need the right tools for the job. This includes glassware and barware.

For glassware, any well-stocked gin bar should include the following variations: Collins, highball, and old-fashioned tumblers; coupe, fizz, rocks, shot, martini, champagne, and bubble wine glasses.

As for barware, equip yourself with a shaker, strainer, mixing glass, bottles for bitters, paring knife, stirring spoons, cocktail thermometer, muddler, jiggers (from ½ oz. to 2 oz. measures), bar towel, wine and champagne stoppers, ice cube trays, and an ice scoop.

coupe

highball

stirring spoons

bottle for bitters

bar towels

martini

strainer

ice scoop

fizz

jigger

shot

muddler

Collins

mixing glass

cocktail thermometer

rocks

ice cube trays

wine and champagne stopper

shaker

bubble wine glass

champagne

pairing knife

How to Convert a Vodka Drinker to a Gin Sipper

(This article is provided by Erik Holzherr, owner of Wisdom, Church & State, and Atlas Arcade, Washington, D.C.)

Simply put, I am a gin drinker. My first bar that I opened up specializes in gin, and much of our cocktail menu is gin heavy. Although up until the 1940s no one had really had a vodka in the US, vodka sales overtook gin sales in 1967 and unfortunately it still remains king. Gin has crept up recently in popularity due the cocktail resurgence and revival of classic tipples, but all too often I have new customers come into one of my bars with an unjust skepticism and fear of the iconic spirit. I have made it my mission in life to convert bland-vodka drinkers into gin enthusiasts. Whenever we are successful in Wisdom, we actually have a bell that we ring at the bar: "An angel gets its gin," or something like that.

The Conversion Process (in 6 easy steps):

Step 1. Demonstrate that you are an SME (Subject Matter Expert).

If you plan to convince people and show them the light, you have to display credibility—otherwise, why should they consider your opinion at all? A convincing statement such as the following might do the trick: "As a professional drunk/bartender, I have tried my fair share of vodka and gin. . . ."

Step 2. Listen to your customer.

Ask, "Why don't you like gin?" then listen to their concerns and possible rant. Be polite—then be prepared to rebut every point they make.

Point: "I got really sick on gin one time in college."

Rebuttal: "Chances are you were drinking cold-compound or cheap gin. Cheap spirits (and their impurities) of any kind, as well as dehydration, are the predominant causes for hangovers."

Point: "I don't like the taste of pine!"

Rebuttal: "Gin tastes like Christmas and everybody loves Christmas! Besides, there is a flavor-profile range of gin that many people aren't aware of."

Point: "Gin makes me think of my grandma."

Rebuttal: "Your grandma sounds cool."

Step 3. Educate.

Explain that gin is just flavored vodka—it must have juniper berry flavoring, but often has a list of other interesting botanicals as well. Vodka, which translates as "little water," tends to disappear in a drink; if I made you a rail vodka cranberry versus a premium vodka cranberry, I would bet you would be unable to tell the difference. Whereas gin, on the other hand, when paired successfully can make a drink "pop" and be more interesting.

Talk about gin's range and cite examples of juniper-heavy brands as well as more floral and balanced brands.

Step 4. Prove to them the beauty of gin.

For the novice, start with a more floral "New Western Style" gin where the juniper doesn't overwhelm. Also you can start simple: try making them a traditional vodka drink with a good gin, such as a gin screwdriver. This keeps the customer in their comfort zone a bit.

Step 5. Reinforce to show gin's versatility.

If they stomach their first gin concoction, make them a different drink using the same gin as the "control group" that already worked, and display how the botanicals accentuate the drink in a different manifestation.

Step 6. The last resort.

When all else fails, punch them in the nose.

CATALOG *of* GIN DISTILLERS

his section is incomplete. I began researching gin distilleries with the idea to include all known makers in this catalog. But the more one searches, the more apparent it becomes that there are many hard-to-find distilleries out there that are just beginning production, or are making gin in extremely small craft batches, or only have local distribution. These factors, combined with limited web presence and lack of a central resource, make it difficult to pinpoint all existing gins. Every time I ventured to a new city I was exposed to a whole new distilling community and found labels I had not yet heard of.

Some independent distilleries have achieved national distribution, such as Portland's House Spirits Distillery (Aviation), which even has a retail shop at the Portland International Airport. But more commonly, newer start-ups may only be available in their surrounding region, such as New Columbia Distillers (Green Hat) whose current reach only includes some states near their home base of Washington, DC. While I have seen Aviation in Philadelphia (my hometown), I had not heard of semi-local Green Hat until I ventured down to DC, a mere two-and-a-half hour drive from Philadelphia.

The fact is, with the number of start-up distilleries appearing every year (if not every month), it's virtually impossible to create a complete up-to-date catalog of gin makers. In addition, some gins are difficult to pinpoint and do not provide distillery information, in which case auxiliary contact information is provided below. And yet this expansive catalog does include an amazing variety of gins, and some genevers, produced by everyone from large corporate distilleries, to small up-and-comers, to those pushing the boundaries of gin's bright future.

35 Maple Street

Sonoma, California
www.35maplestreet.com

This small-batch gin is inspired by the bounty of the garden and by native Tuscan cuisine. Its flavor profile includes cucumber, lemon, sage, and lavender in addition to juniper.

LABEL:
Uncle Val's Gin

A.van Wees Distillery de Ooievaar

Amsterdam, Netherlands
www.de-ooievaar.nl/english

Dating all the way back to its opening in 1782, this is said to be the last standing authentic gin and geneva (genever) producer still in existence in Amsterdam today.

LABELS:
Jonge Wees
Klarenaer
Roggenaer
Taainagel
Old Geneva
Very Old Geneva
Rembrandt Korewijn
Loyaal
Loyaal 5 Year, matured on wood
Roggenaer 3 Year, matured on wood
Very Old Geneva 10 Year, matured on wood
Very Old Geneva 15 Year, matured on wood
Pure Malt 3 Year, matured on wood
Roggenaer 15 Year
Very Old van Wees 20 Year, matured on wood
Three Corner Dry Gin

ADNAMS DISTILLERY

Southwold, England
www.adnams.co.uk

This small-batch distillery opened its doors in 2010. In addition to their main product line, the team welcomes guests to take part in their "Make Your Own Gin" experience utilizing the company's four miniature copper stills.

LABELS:

Adnams Copper House Distilled Gin
Adnams Copper House First Rate Gin

ALTAMAR BRANDS

Corona Del Mar, California
www.rightgin.com

Imported from Sweden, Right Gin uses
nearby Lake Bolmen as its water source
and corn as its grain source, adding
a touch of sweetness to the gin.

LABEL:
Right Gin

ANCHOR DISTILLING COMPANY (DISTRIBUTOR)

San Francisco, California
www.anchordistilling.com

Since 1996, Junipero has been enjoyed as a classic
distilled dry gin, using over a dozen botanicals.
Located on Potrero Hill in San Francisco,
the distillery utilizes a small copper pot still
for its handcrafted productions.

LABELS:
Junipero
Genevieve Gin

ARCUS-GRUPPEN

Halden, Norway
www.arcus.no/en

Norwegian gin Hammer takes inspiration from the classic
London dry style, and filters spring water through volcanic
rock before the distillation process begins.

LABEL:

Hammer London Dry Gin

AUDEMUS SPIRITS

Cognac, France
www.audemus-spirits.com

The first micro-distillery in Cognac, France, features locally sourced honey and handpicked Spanish pink peppercorns, among other spices.

LABEL:
Pink-Pepper Gin

BAINBRIDGE ORGANIC DISTILLERS

Bainbridge Island, Washington
www.bainbridgedistillers.com

This American distillery sources all of its organically grown botanicals and grains from local family farmers, including fresh-harvested Douglass fir boughs, fennel, and citrus peel.

LABEL:
Bainbridge Heritage Organic Doug Fir Gin

BALLAST POINT BREWING & SPIRITS

San Diego, California
www.ballastpoint.com

This small-batch London dry-style gin is vapor-distilled by head brewer Yuseff Cherney and includes botanicals such as rose petal, fresh coriander, and freshly cracked juniper.

LABELS:
Old Grove Gin
Old Grove Barrel Rested Gin

BeBoDrinks

Dijon, France
www.bebodrinks.com

Originating from a 1945 French recipe, this was once the official gin for the American army stationed in Europe. The botanical lineup includes whole lemons, angelica, saffron, iris root, and fennel seed, which are macerated in pure alcohol before distillation.

LABEL:
Diplôme Dry Gin

BEEFEATER DISTILLERY (JAMES BURROUGH LTD.)

London, England
www.beefeatergin.com

Winner of the 2013 San Francisco World Spirits competition, Beefeater is recognized by many as *the* classic London dry gin and is used as the baseline for comparison in the category. After nearly 200 years of distilling in the UK dating back to 1820, Pernod Ricard acquired Beefeater in 2005.

LABELS:
Hawker's Sloe Gin
Boords
Beefeater London Dry Gin
Beefeater 24 London Dry Gin
Beefeater London Market Limited Edition Gin
Beefeater Summer Edition London Dry Gin
Beefeater Crown Jewel Peerless Premium Gin
Beefeater Wet
Beefeater Burrough's Reserve Oak Rested Gin

BENDISTILLERY

Bend, Oregon
www.bendistillery.com

Established in 1996, this award-winning craft distiller starts with pure Oregon water filtered through Cascade lava rock; its juniper berries are all locally grown.

LABELS:
Crater Lake Gin
Crater Lake Estate Gin
Cascade Mountain Gin

BENEVENTO GLOBAL S.L.

Albolote, Spain
www.coolgin.es
www.gin1211.es

A distillery located in a villa in the foothills of Parque Nacional de Sierra Nevada in Spain. Cool gin is purple; it's not the bottle!

LABELS:
Cool Gin
Gin 1211

BERMONDSEY GIN LIMITED

London, England
www.bermondseygin.com

Founder Christian Jensen was inspired by his time spent in Japan
and the "naked martinis" his favorite bartender, Oda-San,
made him nightly—made from a bottle whose faded label
barely read "don Gin." Upon finding out he'd been drinking
a gin no longer in production, he set out to create a throwback
to that antique-style London dry gin that was popular in
nineteenth and early twentieth centuries.

LABELS:
Jensen's London-Distilled Dry Bermondsey Gin
Jensen London-Distilled Old Tom Gin

BERRY BROS. & RUDD

London, England
www.no3gin.com

Using only six botanicals, including sweet Spanish orange peel, Moroccan coriander seed, and cardamom pods, this gin aims to provide the quintessential London dry "Taste of Tradition."

LABEL:
No. 3 St. James London Dry Gin

BERKSHIRE MOUNTAIN DISTILLERS, INC.

Great Barrington, Massachusetts
www.berkshiremountaindistillers.com

This small-batch distillery prides itself on releasing different batches of Ethereal Gin, highlighting unique botanicals such as honeysuckle, rose hips, and clove.

LABELS:

Greylock Gin
Ethereal Gin
Barrel-Aged Ethereal Gin

BEVELAND DISTILLERS

Girona, Spain
www.beveland.com

Beveland is responsible for representing three distinct London dry varieties, including Jodhpur, which is distilled in England.

LABELS:

Jodhpur Imported London Dry Gin
Ginbery's London Dry Gin
Perigan's London Dry Gin

BICARDI USA INC.

Coral Gables, Florida
www.bacardiusa.com

When Don Facundo Bacardî Masso began distilling rum in 1862 in Santiago de Cuba, little did he know that his Bicardi brand would also become one of the largest gin producers in the world. Besides its own-produced labels, Bicardi represents a large catalog of gins from a variety of distilleries.

LABELS:
Bombay Dry
Bombay Sapphire
Bombay Sapphire East
Bosford Gin
Oxley Classic English Gin
(London) Gin

THE BITTER TRUTH

Pullach, Germany
www.the-bitter-truth.com

Pink Gin boasts a juniper-forward yet calm taste; Sloe Gin takes advantage of the fresh sloe berries that grow native in Southern Germany for a dry, semi-sweet drink.

LABELS:
Pink Gin
Sloe Gin

BLACK FOREST DISTILLERS GMBH

Baden-Württemberg, Germany
www.monkey47.com

Hailing from the Black Forest in Germany, Monkey 47 starts with soft water from deep sandstone springs and is distilled with 47 botanicals.

LABELS:

Monkey 47 Schwarzwald Dry Gin
Monkey 47 Schwarzwald Sloe Gin
Monkey 47 Distiller's Cut Schwarzwald Dry Gin

BLACKWOOD'S DISTILLERY

Shetland, Scotland
www.blackwoodsgin.co.uk

Located off the northern coast of Scotland, Blackwood's uses a traditional copper still and infuses its gin with botanicals including lime and coriander.

LABELS:
Blackwood's Vintage Dry Gin
Blackwood's 60% Vintage Dry Gin

BLANC GASTRONOMY

Cadiz, Spain
www.blancgastronomy.com

Blanc uses sea beans—labeled as seaweed—in its distillate, resulting in a uniquely flavored gin.

LABEL:
Blanc Ocean Gin

BLOOMSBURY WINE & SPIRIT

London, England

Although these gins are mysterious, with no website and little information available online about their maker, they are known to be juniper- and citrus-forward gins.

LABELS:
Bloomsbury 45 Original Gin
Bloomsbury 45 Lemon Flavour London Dry Gin
Bloomsbury 45 Orange Flavour Gin

BLUE FLAME SPIRITS

Prosser, Washington
www.blueflamespirits.com

Founded in 2009, settled at the base of Washington's Horse Heaven Hills, this distiller only uses ingredients sourced from a forty-five mile radius, supporting local farmers and assuring quality.

LABELS:
Blue Flame Gin
Blue Flame Ultra Premium Gin

BLUEWATER ORGANIC DISTILLING

EVERETT, WASHINGTON
WWW.BLUEWATERDISTILLING.COM

LABEL:
Halcyon Organic Distilled Gin

The Washington State spirit scene is a bustling one, with many new distilleries opening their doors regularly. I had not heard of many of them until I stopped in a liquor store in neighboring Portland, Oregon, while on the research trail. There were so many brands I had not seen or heard of that I quickly shot pictures of each unknown bottle for further investigation. As I researched these brands that evening, I began noticing that a significant portion of them were produced in Washington State. I knew I couldn't add a destination to my trip but decided to reach out by phone to one distillery that caught my eye—Bluewater Organic Distilling. I was lucky enough to receive a return call from founder John Lundin, a man with a passion for gin who welds his own machinery in-house, including custom fire-boxes for his still, and supports the organic and local markets.

The first thing I ask Lundin about is the vast quantity of distillers I recently discovered all calling Washington home. He tells me, "I think there is something about the Northwest, and maybe Washington in particular, that is incredibly inspiring for entrepreneurial adventures like this. Our legacy with wineries and breweries has really set the stage for the craft-distilling side of the world. Lots of stuff happening."

"And what is the distillery scene like? Is it more communal or is there a competitive edge to it?" I ask. John answers, "It's mostly very communal. I think there are some growing pains. As this industry finds its maturity I think we have some bugs to work out, but in general it's a great group. I don't know how familiar you are with the intricacies of the craft law" (I am not), "but being a gin writer I think you can appreciate some of the complexities. The craft law that was put into effect in Washington, which stimulated a lot of distilling, is actually incredibly restrictive, or actually almost prohibitive, for making a world-class gin. So there's a lot of gin lovers, like me and the guys who make Voyager gin and the Big Gin guys, we're all very adamant to make the legislative side much more inclusive to the different craft approaches, not just whiskey from local barley."

"What type of still does Bluewater use?" I ask. John replies, "We're using hand-hammered copper alembic stills that are direct-fired. So we're literally putting flame underneath the kettles. These stills have eight centuries of tradition. They go back to the 1200s—the alchemists in the Arabic world, in Europe with the Moorish conquest, the monks were working with them for a couple hundred years. Gin, as it evolved in about 1600, really rests on the shoulders of hundreds of years of distilling with aromatics and these types of alembic stills."

"What other factors besides the still do you have to consider when preparing to create a gin?" I ask. John tells me, "In America we're blessed with incredible water everywhere, compared with a lot of parts of the world. But when it comes to spirits production, I think you end up having to do a lot of doctoring to the water to really have a good foundation for blending with spirits. I know a lot of distillers can get around a lot of the flavor profiles by just using reverse osmosis. I'm kind of a minimalist in many ways and if I have the ability to source an exquisite water supply and do very little to it, it becomes a very important contributing character. It's this wonderful ability to allow the water to contribute to the flavors.

Our water here has a really nice balanced sweetness and incredible crisp character. Our fresh water supply is from a reservoir at an elevation in the middle of the Cascades and we're getting 165 inches of rainfall per year on top of all the snowmelt. It's an incredible water supply."

Noting the importance of using a superb water source, I ask about the significance of sourcing all organic unadulterated goods. John tells me, "This is a big one for me. As an industry—whether we're the producers, the suppliers, the consumers—we don't demand very much from our spirits, and that's something that I hope changes in the next five to ten years because, when it comes to wine and spirits, we do not demand much on the sustainability side. For me the organic side is very important. I believe it puts me in contact with the finest grains on the planet, the finest aromatics on the planet, and I think that shines through at the end of the day when we pop the cork on the bottle."

"The craft law that was put into effect in Washington, which stimulated a lot of distilling, is actually incredibly restrictive, or actually almost prohibitive, for making a world-class gin."

"Is it difficult to go fully organic?" I ask. "It's hard to get organic certified. It's a big cost commitment. The raw materials are going to cost anywhere from two to four to six times higher than commodity materials. We use no genetically engineered products. There's a lot of transparency that's starting to be demanded from consumers on what's in their food. So I feel like we're on the right side of a lot of arguments," John says.

"Is it more important that the ingredients are organic certified or that they come from a local producer?" I ask. "Gin, in its classic form, is a product of the spice trade and ships running from Asia and back. For many flavors, like the cassia bark, you really only get that out of Southeast Asia. I made a very conscious decision to commit myself more to organics and responsible sourcing at every turn, rather than forcing myself to source hyper-local. I respect that and I wish I could do both, but you really can't do both right now. I'm kind of a purest at heart, and I didn't want to make a gin that expressed what's growing in the back yard. I wanted to express a London dry style in a very fine way. When you do that you start pulling citrus elements and root elements that maybe don't come locally. That said, maybe half my aromatics are grown in Oregon. I keep it as close as I can!"

I also know, from their website, that their products are housed in American-made glass bottles, which is of great importance to the Bluewater Company. John explains, "Using American-made glass is a big one for me. I have nothing against China as an industrial center, but I do feel like, on a political and economic side, we kind of blew it with the economy and we outsourced way too much at the expense of our own American industries. My ability to finally source American-made glass exclusively is my subtle commentary on the outsourcing."

As I take my phone off speaker and raise it to my ear to say goodbye, John gives me one final piece of insight. "Here's one thing a lot of gin distillers don't mention. When you distill a gin, your aromatic distillation is most often a concentrated form—gin concentrate. What most distilleries do is add neutral spirits to find the right blend or proportions. Every drop of neutral spirit that gets blended into Halcyon is finished distilled in an alembic. So we're able to remove those lingering heads that exist in all neutral spirits. We're able to remove them on both halves, not just the gin and aromatic side but also what we blend back in."

> "As an industry—whether we're the producers, the suppliers, the consumers— we don't demand very much from our spirits, and that's something that I hope changes in the next five to ten years. . . ."

John Lundin gave me a great perspective on both the current and upcoming American gin landscape. Even by crafting a traditional London dry in America, Bluewater has created something new and classic at the same time—an American-London dry. It's something truly unique and historically inspired, and that's what's it's all about.

Boë

Doune, Scotland
www.boe-gin.com

Boë gin is fashioned in a unique Carterhead still via a vapor-infusion technique. Cassia bark, almonds, ginger, licorice, and cubeb berries are some of the botanicals used in this production.

LABEL:
Boë Superior Gin

BORCO

Hamburg, Germany
www.borco.com

Borco represents a unique collection of spirit brands, including two gins and many jenevers.

LABELS:
Finsbury Platinum Gin 47%
Finsbury Distilled London Dry Gin
De Kuyper Jenever
Rutte Jenever Oude 12
Rutte Jenever Oude Simon
Rutte Jenever Paradyswyn

THE BOTANICAL'S

Orihuela, Spain
www.thebotanicalsgin.com

This distillery takes its time producing gin, distilling each botanical separately for varying amounts of time, blending them, and distilling one final time.

LABEL:
The Botanical's Premium London Dry Gin

BOTTLED BY CADENHEAD'S

Campbeltown, Scotland
www.wmcadenhead.com

Although most well-known for their range of whiskies, Cadenhead's is also making a name for itself with its saffron-infused gin, which has a notable yellowish tint.

LABELS:
Cadenhead's Old Raj Blue Label Gin
Cadenhead's Old Raj Red Label Gin
Cadenhead's Classic Gin
Cadenhead's Sloe Gin

BRAMLEY AND GAGE

Thornbury, Gloucestershire, UK
www.sixoclockgin.co.uk

Dedicated to providing the makings for the perfect gin & tonic,
Bramley and Gage also produce Six O'clock tonic,
made with natural quinine.

LABELS:
Six O'clock Gin
Bramley & Gage Sloe Gin
Bramley & Gage Organic Sloe Gin
Bramley & Gage Damson Gin

BREUCKELEN DISTILLING

Brooklyn, New York
www.brkdistilling.com

Focusing on farm-to-bottle production, Breuckelen uses only New York-harvested grains and sees their product through from milling, mashing, and fermenting the grains to labeling the bottles.

LABEL:
Glorious Gin

BROCKMANS

Surrey, England
www.brockmansgin.com

Using Bulgarian coriander and Valencia oranges as two components of the flavor profile, Brockmans encourages its patrons to enjoy their gin lone over ice.

LABEL:
Brockmans Gin

BROKER'S

Surrey, England
www.brokersgin.com

With an obvious sense of humor, Broker's adorns all their bottles with a black bowler hat for a cap. In 2013 Broker's was certified kosher by Kashrut Division-London Beth Din.

LABEL:

Broker's Premium London Dry Gin

BRUICHLADDICH DISTILLERY

Isle of Islay Argyll, Scotland
www.bruichladdich.com

While using traditional flavors such as orris root and coriander seed, The Botanist also integrates 22 locally sourced, handpicked botanicals.

LABELS:
The Botanist
The London Gin

BULLDOG IMPORTS

Manhasset, New York
www.bulldoggin.com

Winner of numerous awards, including the Top 50 Spirit award, this gin is crafted at an English distillery with over 250 years of gin-making under its belt.

LABEL:
Bulldog London Dry Gin

BUTLER'S GIN

London, England
www.butlersgin.co.uk

Ross William Butler crafts his gin
with forward notes of lemongrass
and cardamom, using ingredients
and techniques that promote
a sustainable environment.

LABEL:
Butler's Gin

CALEDONIA SPIRITS

Hardwick, Vermont
www.caledoniaspirits.com

A unique gin that lets raw northern
honey shine; the honey is added
just before bottling.

LABELS:
Barr Hill Gin
Barr Hill Reserve

THE CAMBRIDGE DISTILLERY

Cambridge, England
www.cambridgedistillery.co.uk

In addition to the always changing, extremely small-batch Cambridge label, Japanese Gin merges London and Japan including traditional botanicals alongside shiso leaf, sesame seeds, and sanshō.

LABELS:
Cambridge Gin
Japanese Gin

Captive Spirits

Seattle, Washington
www.captivespiritsdistilling.com

Created by third-generation distiller Ben Capdevielle,
Big Gin is distilled in a 100-gallon Vendome pot still
and contains notes of orange and juniper.

LABELS:
Big Gin
Bourbon Barreled Big Gin

Cascade Peak Spirits

Ashland, Oregon
www.organicnationspirits.com

With a focus on supporting Oregon's local commerce, this producer begins with organic rye, wheat, and corn, and is certified organic.

LABEL:
Organic Nation Gin

CASK LIQUID MARKETING

London, England
www.caskliquidmarketing.com

As a spirit agency, Cask makes three gin labels available.
Gin Mare is a Mediterranean take utilizing botanicals such
as Arbequina olives, basil, rosemary, and thyme.

LABELS:
Cremorne 1859 Colonel Fox's Cremorne London Distilled Dry Gin
Cremorne 1859 Gentleman Badger's Wild Blackthorn Sloe Gin
Gin Mare

CHASE DISTILLERY

Hereford, England
www.chasedistillery.co.uk

Chase is a family-owned distillery located on an English farm.
They began producing vodka in 2008 from the farm's potatoes,
and soon moved into creating gins using a spirit-base made
with organic cider apples from their orchard.

LABELS:
Williams Chase Elegant Gin
Williams Chase Gb Extra Dry Gin
Williams Seville Orange Gin
Chase Summer Fruit Cup

COGNAC FERRAND USA

Ars, France
www.cognacferrand.com

As the name implies, Cognac Ferrand began with cognac, but soon moved into producing gin and rum. Citadelle gin employs 19 botanicals including jasmine, honeysuckle, grains of paradise, and cinnamon. Botanicals are infused for 72 hours before a 12-hour distillation run through a copper pot still.

LABELS:
Citadelle Gin
Citadelle Reserve Gin
Magellan Gin

COPPER FIDDLE DISTILLERY

Lake Zurich, Illinois
www.copperfiddledistillery.com

This small-batch producer uses an American-made multi-plate column still to vapor-infuse the botanicals that are stored in a gin basket at the top of the column during distillation.

LABELS:

Fiddle Gin
Tom Gin

COPPER FOX DISTILLERY

Sperryville, Virginia
www.copperfox.biz

A gin produced from 100-percent malted barley. Depending on what's growing in their garden, sippers can expect to find subtle variations between each small batch.

LABEL:

Copper Fox VirGin

THE CORNISH GIN DISTILLERY LIMITED

Cornwall, England
www.cornishgin.co.uk

Using Cornish spring water, this gin is made in a traditional copper still using the one-shot distillation method.

LABEL:
Elemental Cornish Gin

Corsair Artisan, LLC

Nashville, Tennessee
www.corsairartisan.com

A small-batch gin crafted in a hand-hammered gin-head pot still. *Gin-head: (n.)* the basket that botanicals are placed in above the boiler. As vapor rises and passes through it, the basket absorbs essential oils.

LABELS:
Corsair Gin
Corsair Barrel Aged Gin

Craft Distillers

Ukiah, California
www.craftdistillers.com

Using a wheat-based grain-neutral spirit, Russell Henry gin is created exercising both infusion and distillation processes. Owner Crispin Cain currently produces two variations on his London dry—one including the fruit and leaves of the *limau purut*, a Malaysian lime; the other sourcing organic Hawaiian ginger from Kauai.

LABELS:
Russell Henry Gin London Dry
Russell Henry Gin Malaysian Limes
Russell Henry Gin Hawaiian White Ginger

CROP HARVEST EARTH CO

New York, New York
www.farmersgin.com

With a concentration on creating a stellar certified-organic gin and supporting a sustainable community, Farmer's states that its desire is to make a gin that is "better for the Earth as well as better for flavor."

LABEL:
Farmer's Gin

DEATH'S DOOR SPIRITS

Middleton, Wisconsin
www.deathsdoorspirits.com

Located on an island that houses a mere 700 year-round tenants, the company donates one percent of annual revenue to organizations protecting the Great Lakes.

LABEL:
Death's Door Gin

DESERT JUNIPER GIN

Bend, Oregon
www.handcraftedgin.com

Starting with mountain spring water, natural grains,
and handpicked wild juniper berries, this gin is
filtered through native crushed lava rock.

LABEL:

Desert Juniper Gin

DIAGEO

London, England
www.diageo.com

This business represents some of the most-consumed and widely distributed spirit labels in the world. While many are large-batch productions, they also have some smaller labels in their portfolio.

LABELS:
Tanqueray
Tanqueray 10
Tanqueray Special Dry Gin
Tanqueray Rangpur
Gordon's Gin
Gordon's Sloe Gin
Gordon's Gin & Tonic
Space
Spark
Booth's Gin

DISTILLERY
NO. 209

San Francisco, California
www.distillery209.com

This small-batch kosher-certified gin
highlights botanicals such as lemon, orange,
bergamot, and coriander. The distillery
is located on San Francisco's Pier 50 and
claims to be the "only distillery in
the world built over water!"

LABEL:
No 209 Gin

DOGWOOD
DISTILLING

Forest Grove, Oregon
www.dogwooddistilling.com

Union Gin is double-distilled from 100
percent American grain in small batches.

LABEL:
Union Gin

DOMAINE PINNACLE

Quebec, Canada
www.domainepinnacle.com/en

Hailing from Canada, Ungava infuses handpicked botanicals
specific to their region including cloudberry (a member
of the *Rosaceae* family), Labrador tea and crowberry
(both members of the *Ericaceae* family), and Nordic juniper.

LABEL:
Ungava Premium Dry Gin

DRY FLY DISTILLING

Spokane, Washington
www.dryflydistilling.com

As New York World Wine & Spirit Competition's gold medal winner in 2011, Dry Fly uses only raw materials grown by sustainable local farms.

LABEL:
Dry Fly Gin

THE DUKE DESTILLERIE

Munich, Germany
www.theduke-gin.de

Using a copper kettle, Duke Gin—named in honor of the Duke of Bavaria—includes 13 herbs and spices including coriander, angelica root, lavender, ginger root, orange blossom, and cubeb pepper.

LABEL:
The Duke Munich Dry Gin

EDGERTON DISTILLERS LTD.

London, England
www.edgertonpink.com

Billed as the sole modern London-based pink gin producer, Edgerton produces their take on a historical favorite of the Royal Navy. The juice derives its pink color from added bitters.

LABEL:
Edgerton Pink Gin

ELEPHANT GIN

Hamburg, Germany
www.elephant-gin.com

A unique German gin that utilizes botanicals native to Africa, such as baobab, the buchu plant, and devil's claw. Because an African elephant is killed every fifteen minutes, the fight to end unrestrained ivory poaching is the founding centerpiece of Elephant Gin, and 15 percent of all company profits are donated to Big Life Foundation and Space for Elephants.

LABEL:
Elephant Gin

English Spirit Distillery

Cambridgeshire, England
www.englishvodkacompany.com

This gin begins with their house-made base spirit and ends with their suggestion for enjoyment—put crushed ice into a glass, add two salted capers, pour in Dr. J's.

LABELS:
Dr. J's Gin
Rose Petal Gin

FEW SPIRITS

Evanston, Illinois
www.fewspirits.com

As 2011's *International Review of Spirits'* silver medal winner, Few has come a long way. The town of Evanston had been a dry town dating back to 1858, ending when city council voted to allow the serving of alcohol in hotels and restaurants in 1972, but distilling wasn't legalized until later.

LABELS:
Few American Gin
Few Barrel Aged Gin

FILLIERS DISTILLERY

Deinze, Belgium
www.filliers.be

Filliers began creating jeneveres, the precursor to gin,
based on a recipe from 1880. Wheat, rye, and malt are distilled
and aged for three years in oak barrels before being
blended with their juniper berry distillate.

LABELS:
Filliers Dry Gin 28
Filliers Dry Gin 28 "Tangerine Seasonal Edition"
Filliers Dry Gin 28 Sloe Gin
Filliers Barrel Aged Dry Gin
Filliers 30° Jenever
Old Jenever 5 Year
Old Jenever 8 Year
Old Jenever 12 Year
Filliers Jonge Jenever
Apple Jonge Jenever
Lemon Jonge Jenever
Redcurrant Jonge Jenever
Passion Fruits Jonge Jenever
Cherries Jonge Jenever
Pomelo Jonge Jenever
Apple and Kiwi Jonge Jenever
Cuberdon Jonge Jenever
Chocolate Cream Jenever
Vanilla Cream Jenever
Speculoos Cream Jenever
Banana Cream Jenever
Coconut Cream Jenever
Amaretto Cream Jenever

FINGER LAKES DISTILLING

Burdett, New York

www.fingerlakesdistilling.com

Using a base spirit comprised of 75 percent fermented grapes, Finger Lakes creates a fundamentally different take on gin.

LABELS:

Seneca Drums Gin

Mackenzie Distiller's Reserve Gin

FOXDENTON ESTATE COMPANY LTD.

Buckingham, England
www.foxdentonestate.co.uk

A company that likes to experiment with fruit-based spirits built on top of a gin base, they also offer limited personalized runs with custom-engraved bottles.

LABELS:
Foxdenton 48 Gin
Foxdenton Sloe Gin
Foxdenton Raspberry Gin
Foxdenton Winslow Plum Gin
Foxdenton Damson Gin
Tottering Gin
Tottering Sloe Gin

FREMONT MISCHIEF

Seattle, Washington
www.fremontmischief.com

Using organic and heirloom grains sourced
from neighboring Whidbey Island, this
distillery keeps it local and fresh.

LABEL:
Fremont Mischief Gin

G&J GREENALL

Cheshire, England
www.gjgreenall.co.uk

With a heritage dating back to 1761,
Greenall distills its own in-house labels
and also bottles beverages for other
distillers, making them the world's
second-largest gin producer.

LABELS:
Greenall's Original London Dry Gin
Berkeley Square Gin
Bloom Gin

G&J DISTILLERS

Cheshire, England
www.opihr.com

This oriental-spiced London dry style gin, inspired by the ancient Spice Route, uses a botanical profile including spicy cubeb berries from Indonesia, black pepper from India, and coriander from Morocco.

LABEL:
Opihr Gin

GABRIEL BOUDIER DIJON

Dijon, France
www.boudier.com

Dating back to 1874, this distiller recommends a *La saveur Boudier* cocktail, made with 50ml (1.7 oz.) Saffron gin, 25ml (0.8 oz.) cinnamon syrup, and crushed pear.

LABELS:
Boudier Dry Gin
Boudier Saffron Gin

GENIUS LIQUIDS

AUSTIN, TEXAS

WWW.GENIUSLIQUIDS.COM

LABELS:

Genius Standard Gin

Genius Navy Strength Gin

Genius Liquids, owned and operated by Mike Groener, is an exemplary model of an innovative distillery emerging on the American gin frontier. Mike was kind enough to take an hour to discuss gin, his young distillery, and the future of "Western gin," a relatively new term used to denote a new American style of gin production.

"You have no idea how much I love talking about gin!" Groener tells me as we begin our discussion. "Sounds like I've got the right guy!" I reply.

I am interested in Genius Liquids because, as a fledgling company, they offer a fresh perspective and are inspired by, but not bound by, classic tradition. "How long have you been selling your gin?" I ask. "We've been to market seventy-five days now, not a long time, but we've gotten a really great response. I think people have been supportive of the fact that we are doing this the hard way—handmade. We've taken about a year and a half to work on the recipe, including many disrupted nights' sleep. I lost a lot of sleep!"

"Why gin?" I ask. "For us, it was the fact that gin stands for something," Mike states. "It's not neutral. You have to have a perspective, right? If you don't, you're making vodka. That's why for us it's more of a rally against vodka than it is a proponent of gin. We just want it to stand for something and try to give people a pleasurable experience with gin they may not have had before." In addition to their main label (45% ABV), Genius also produces a navy strength gin (57% ABV) for use in a stronger tipple.

"For us it's more of a rally against vodka than it is a proponent of gin."

I had previously read about Genius's two-stage process, consisting of a round of infusion and then a round of distillation, which is one popular method. "What distilling practices does Genius employ to create a gin that has the potential to appeal to nontraditional gin lovers?" I ask. Mike tells me, "We really just took the hard way. For an un-aged spirit, we're not aging it, but we definitely took another five to seven days to do the following process for the flavor. We do everything ourselves. Fermentation from scratch takes about seven days, and then we have this 16–17% ABV wash, this liquid. Then we go and do our initial stripping run and that creates essentially the vodka. We have the neutral spirit that we then steep with a fine mesh bag full of elderflower, lavender, lime leaf, lime peel, rosehips, a little bit of angelica root, and I think one other thing we put in there." I remember from other conversations with distillers that the reason this is usually done is because many botanicals change character—are dulled or unpleasantly altered—when heated to the point that alcohol turns to vapor in the still.

Mike continues, "What we're able to do, in my opinion, is impart the best layers at the right temperature. We do steeping of certain ingredients at room temperature and then we take this really nice green herbaceous liquid and distill it again with our column-still ingredients, which are vapor-infused, such as cardamom and juniper, which respond really well to heat." I remark that it's a lengthy process and ask Mike to explain why it is worth the added effort. "When we look at gin, I think it is important to a degree to cover some of the distinctions of how things are processed. Seagram's is a great example, adding certain oils at the very end, essences, a copy of a copy if you will. Most of the smaller guys are taking a natural handmade approach to it, without added oils, hopefully without charcoal filtering and these kinds of things."

> "When we look at gin, I think it is important to a degree to cover some of the distinctions of how things are processed."

"What do you think of the term 'Western gin' that has begun to pop up when classifying some American gins?" I ask. Mike says, "To think that the US and Canada have created a new niche in the market of gin, I think it's cool even though I don't think Genius fits in the category. Gins like Aviation, Death's Door, Smalls, and Voyager really fit in with Western-style gin and created a new market out of it."

It was a pleasure to speak with Mike and get a glimpse of a distillery just placing their first footprint on American soil.

GILBEY DISTILLERY/ BEAM GLOBAL

Deerfield, Illinois
www.beamglobal.com

As the largest US-based spirits company, Beam not only crafts but also markets an ample range of spirits. Invest in gin: NYSE: BEAM.

LABELS:
Gilbey's Special Dry Gin
Larios London Dry Gin
Larios 12 Botanicals Premium Gin

GINSELF

Valencia, Spain
www.ginself.com

In a tribute to the Mediterranean pallet, Ginself uses botanicals such as Mandarin orange blossom and tiger nut.

LABEL:
Ginself

GrandTen Distilling

Boston, Massachusetts
www.grandten.com

Located in a former South Boston iron foundry, GrandTen Distilling is adamant that every step—from selecting the raw ingredients to labeling the bottle—is done by hand.

LABELS:
Wire Works American Gin
Wire Works Special Reserve Gin

GREEN BOX DRINKS LTD.

London, England
www.boxergin.com

As a London dry style gin, Boxer incorporates fresh bergamot,
nutmeg, cinnamon, and licorice root in addition
to wild Himalayan juniper.

LABEL:

Boxer Gin

GREENBAR CRAFT DISTILLERY

Los Angeles, California
www.greenbar.biz

Dating back to a sixteenth-century distilling technique, it takes two months for Greenbar to craft their gin.

LABEL:
Tru Organic Gin

GREENHOOK GINSMITHS

BROOKLYN, NEW YORK

WWW.GREENHOOKGIN.COM

LABELS:

American Dry Gin

Beach Plum Gin Liqueur

Steven DeAngelo opened the doors to the Greenhook Ginsmiths distillery in 2012 in Brooklyn, New York. After a departure from his career on Wall Street, he began walking the long and complex path toward opening a distillery and crafting his recipes. "Like opening any business in New York," Steven tells me, "there are so many various levels of bureaucracy to get through." But he succeeded.

Steven was gracious enough to invite me to tour his Brooklyn facility in the spring of 2013. Upon entering, I notice a stunning still that takes up a large portion of one wall. Along another wall are dozens of bottles of Greenhook's seasonal Beach Plum Gin Liqueur getting readied for labeling. Steven looks at the bottle-labeling machine in frustration and tells me that he's had it for over six months and it is still not working properly. Because of this, he chooses to label every bottle by hand and hopes that the manufacturer can get it working soon.

I ask Steven about the inspiration behind the Beach Plum Gin Liqueur. "We wanted to do a traditional English sloe gin. What I didn't realize initially is that sloes don't actually grow in North America. I found a farmer in England that had a lot of sloes on his property, but he was a dairy farmer and didn't have post-harvesting techniques, which

Steven DeAngelo.

"In this country, it's not like you can just go and work in a distillery and learn how to be a distiller."

allow you to chill the fruit down to the pit to preserve for shipping. There was a good chance that by the time they showed up at customs, they would be molded and ruined. I scrapped the idea. But then I remembered seeing beach plums when I was a kid out in the Rockaways [off of Long Island, New York], but I never realized that they were a very close relative of the sloe. They call the sloe a sloe berry, but it's really a wild plum. They [beach plums] only actually grow from Maryland up to Maine on the Atlantic Coast. I thought it was a cool local spin on a sloe gin."

Considering his background on Wall Street, I ask him the most basic question, "How did you learn to make gin?"

"In this country, it's not like you can just go and work in a distillery and learn how to be a distiller. Everything is pretty much self-taught. We probably went through ten, twelve [combinations] just finding the exact botanical profile we wanted to use. That's nothing compared to actually finding the right *amount* of each botanical to use. We went through probably anywhere from seventy-five to one-hundred runs finalizing that recipe. It's really more about the balance of the botanicals together."

I remember reading about Steven's unique mercury vacuum-sealed still, and ask him to elaborate.

"Our still is one of our most unique aspects. We operate under a vacuum seal. That's the key reason we have such an aromatic and full-flavored gin. Two of the key ingredients in our gin are flowers—chamomile and elderflower—which create a very beautiful aroma, which you couldn't really do under traditional distillation practice. The heat associated with traditional distillation would burn off a lot of the delicate aromas from flowers. Flowers are very delicate. The capacity of running under a vacuum allows us to distill at lower temperatures and is integral in creating our gin."

I thank Steven for the tour, wise words, and samples, and head out into the Brooklyn summer heat.

> "The capacity of running under a vacuum allows us to distill at lower temperatures and is integral in creating our gin."

G'VINE

Cognac, France
www.g-vine.com

A unique gin in that it's distilled from grapes instead of traditional grains. *Wine Enthusiast* gave both Floraison and Nouaison labels a rating of "superb" (90–95).

LABELS:
G'vine
G'vine Floraison
G'vine Nouaison

HALL & BRAMLEY

Liverpool, England
www.halewood-int.com

Founded in 1978, Halewood International Holdings (as it is known today) rose to become the largest independent drinks manufacture and distributer in the UK.

LABEL:
Belgravia Gin

HAMMER & SON LTD.

Birmingham, England
www.geraniumgin.com
www.oldenglishgin.com

H. Hammer and his father, who was also a chemist, created Geranium gin, which, as the name implies, uses the geranium flower as one of its botanicals.

LABELS:
Germanium Premium London Dry Gin
Old English Gin

HASWELL

London, England
www.haswellgin.co.uk

Spirit developer and owner Julian Haswell set out to craft a gin that would be "unashamedly citrus" and uses botanicals such as bitter orange peel, sweet orange peel, and lemon peel.

LABEL:
Haswell London Distilled Dry Gin

HAYMAN DISTILLERS

East Anglia, England
www.hayman-distillers.co.uk

Hayman produces a wide range of gins and, until 2013 when they installed their own still named "Marjorie," created their gins at Thames Distillery in Clapham, England.

LABELS:
Hayman's London Dry Gin
Hayman's Old Tom Gin
Royal Dock of Deptford Navy Strength Gin
Hayman's 1850 Reserve Gin
Hayman's Sloe Gin
Hayman's Gin Liqueur

HEADFRAME SPIRITS

Butte, Montana

www.headframespirits.com

Named after a zinc mine in Butte, Montana, Anselmo Gin uses 12 botanicals including citrus and huckleberry.

LABEL:

Anselmo Gin

THE HENDRICK'S GIN DISTILLERY LTD., THE GIRVAN DISTILLERY

Girvan, Scotland
www.hendricksgin.com

This was one of the first small-batch gins—distilled in extremely small quantities of 450 liters—to make its way to the States. Part of Hendrick's unique flavor comes from infusing the spirit with rose petal and cucumber.

LABEL:
Hendrick's Gin

HERITAGE DISTILLING CO

Gig Harbor, Washington
www.heritagedistilling.com

Soft gin is one of a small number of gins being distilled from grapes. It won the 2013 Double Gold-Best Gin medal at FiftyBest.com International Tasting in New York.

LABELS:
Soft Gin
Elk Rider Crisp Gin

HERNÖ

Härnösand, Sweden
www.herno.se

Crafting a line of award-winning gins, Hernö's flagship gin is made with botanicals such as lingonberry, meadowsweet, and black pepper.

LABELS:
Hernö Swedish Exellence Gin
Hernö Navy Strength Gin
Hernö Juniper Cask Gin

Adventures in Portland at House Spirits Distillery

PORTLAND, OREGON

WWW.AVIATIONGIN.COM

LABEL:

Aviation American Gin

Let me say that as soon as I arrive in downtown Portland, I have the sense that it is one of the coolest towns I have set foot in. It may be because I came of age in the nineties, but I feel right at home. It has been a while since I have seen so much flannel, or a freestanding phone both, or a show flyer for the Breeders. Everyone looks comfortable and friendly as I walk past the blocks lined by permanent food-truck venders slinging dishes from around the globe.

I venture from my downtown hotel, crossing the Willamette River, to the Southeast side of Portland arriving at a section of SE 7th Avenue, which has incurred the nickname "Distillery Row." I am meeting with Christian Krogstad, founder of House Spirits Distillery, which produces Aviation gin. I enter past a welcome sign into the tasting room that is lined with House Spirits products including a coffee liqueur made with local Stumptown beans, two variations of aquavit, and a malt whiskey. Christian walks in, greets me, and leads the way next door to the distillery. Besides the beauty of the still and the hum of machinery at work, the first thing that catches my eye upon entering is a small kitchen and bar setup on the left-hand side of the room. Christian offers me a seat at the bar to fix me a drink, with Aviation of course. He also pours me a sip of local producer Imbue's Petal & Thorn vermouth after I mention I hadn't gotten a chance to try it yet. (Note: This may have been the first great handcrafted vermouth I had tasted, and it opened my mind to the possibility that maybe I really could like vermouth. That has since been confirmed by multiple brands of quality vermouth.)

In 2006, two years after opening their doors, House Spirits Distillery began producing Aviation American Gin. In collaboration with mixologist extraordinaire Ryan Magarian and co-owner and NFL great Joe Montana, Aviation was born as a "renegade regional gin" with a strong focus on using quality ethically sourced ingredients. After finishing our cocktails we begin to walk deeper into the room, in between giant stills all working their magic. There is a big steel vat waiting to be filled with neutral grain spirit (base spirit) so the gin-creating process can begin. As I glance down, sitting next to the vat I see a small container of yellowish liquid and Christian tells me that's how the base spirit will look after a round of maceration before going into the still for distillation. He explains that he prefers the term "maceration" over "infusion," because infusion confuses some into thinking that no distillation takes place during the entire process of creating Aviation gin. Not the case.

Like many other distilleries today, creating Aviation gin utilizes a multi-stepped process involving maceration and actual distilling. In addition to juniper, Aviation's flavor profile contains lavender, Indian sarsaparilla, cardamom, and anise seed, to name a few. It is worth noting that House Spirits enlists a local resource, the Oregon Spice Company, to

seek out botanicals from all over the world and provide them for use in Aviation gin.

After the initial maceration process, where a specially made cloth sack is filled with botanicals and steeped in neutral spirit, it is time to distill. The infused spirit is then transferred into the stainless steel still, where the heat will climax at 173 degrees Fahrenheit causing alcohol to transform to vapor and separate from the other fluids. House Spirits does not use any botanicals in this stage because the purpose of this step is not to impart additional aromatic flavor; the complete botanical flavor profile is infused in the initial maceration stage. Instead, the steel still is used to meld the existing flavors imparted during maceration, refining the existing botanical profile without additional effects. The first vapors, known as the heads, are unwanted and are collected and removed so that the desired middle of the distillate, or the hearts, may be collected for the next step. The end of the distillate, or the tails, are unwanted and discarded as well. Separating the hearts out of the entire distillation process is often referred to as a cut.

Next, pure water is blended with the concentrated spirit to achieve a balanced gin resting at 84 proof. The water/gin blend is allowed to sit for a few days, further integrating all the elements. The final steps are bottling, capping, and labeling. Then it's off for distribution, and House Spirits, out on the forefront of new American gin, has secured some of the best distribution of any independent gin distillery. Southern Wine & Spirits, with a reach of 35 states, signed a deal to distribute Aviation across the US. As Aviation grows in popularity, it shall pave the path for other independent producers—perhaps other Oregon distillers like those pictured here—to attain a wider commercial reach. I thank Christian for his time and bus it back across the river.

HOXTON GIN

London, England
www.hoxtongin.com

This gin strives to be different, as seen in the inclusion of coconut and grapefruit in its infusion.

LABEL:
Hoxton Gin

IAN MACLEOD DISTILLERS

Broxburn, Scotland
www.ianmacleod.com

This large, independent, family producer makes London Hill gin at Langley Distillery. Botanical flavors are extracted by maceration in neutral grain spirit before distillation in a pot still.

LABEL:
London Hill Gin

ICEBERG

St. John's, Canada
www.iceberg.ca

As the name implies, this Canadian take on a London dry style gin sources water from icebergs. To start, the water is blended with neutral grain spirit made from locally harvested sweet corn.

LABEL:
Iceberg London Dry Gin

INDIO SPIRITS

Portland, Oregon
www.indiospirits.com

When distilling his gin, owner John Ufford uses botanicals such as sweet orange peel, paradise seed, and lemongrass.

LABEL:
Cricket Club Gin

Intl. Beverage Holdings Ltd., USA, Inc.

New York, New York
www.interbevgroup.com

Since 2006, this company has been discovering and developing local brands and bringing them to the global market.

LABELS:
Caorunn Gin (Balmenach Distillery, Scotland)
Coldstream London Gin (Inver House Distillers, UK)

IT'S 5 ARTISAN DISTILLERY

Cashmere, Washington
www.fiveoclockdistillery.squarespace.com

Using only Washington-sourced ingredients, It's 5 crafts their gin with botanicals including hibiscus, coriander, cardamom, and star anise.

LABEL:
Northwest Dry Gin

KNOCKEEN HILLS

Canterbury, England
www.heather-gin.com
www.elderflower-gin.com

Featuring a carefully selected bottle and label, Knockeen Hills creates Elderflower gin through a process of five distillations. As a "London Cut" style gin, all the botanicals have been harvested and distilled within London.

LABELS:
Elderflower Gin
Heather Gin

LANGLEY'S

Hampshire, England
www.langleysgin.com

Made with eight botanicals, this gin is distilled in a small English pot still using 100 percent English grain spirit.

LABEL:
Langley's No. 8

LANGTONS OF SKIDDAW

Lakeland, England
www.langtonsgin.co.uk

This distillery's water feeds from an aquifer under a mountain in northern England and is said to be up to a million years old; it filters through black slate that is 400 times older, providing a pure, fresh, crisp flavor.

LABEL:
Langtons No. 1 Gin

LARK DISTILLERY

Tasmania, Australia
www.larkdistillery.com.au

This distillery is named in honor of the founder of the distillery, Bill Lark, who is known as the "godfather" of Australian whisky. Its distinct flavor is derived from the inclusion of the native pepperberry, collected wild from the Tasmanian forest.

LABEL:
Lark's Godfather Tasmanian Gin

LETHERBEE DISTILLERS

Chicago, Illinois
www.letherbee.com

What started out as a hooch-making hobby for bartender Brenton Engel soon gained cult popularity and led to the establishment of this independent artisan distillery. Check out the website for their ever-changing seasonal varieties.

LABELS:

Letherbee Gin
Letherbee Prairie Grass Gin (and other seasonal varieties)

LITTLE BIRD

London, England
www.littlebirdgin.com

A simple, small-batch gin that is "lovingly distilled in London"
to create a citrus-focused yet classic London dry.

LABEL:
Little Bird London Dry Gin

THE LONDON DISTILLERY COMPANY

London, England
www.thelondondistillerycompany.com

The proprietary distilling method begins in "Christina,"
a traditional copper alembic pot; proceeds as delicate botanicals
are added to "Little Albion," a state-of-the-art cold vacuum still;
and completes after several weeks when the infused spirit
is bottled and hand-labeled.

LABEL:
Dodd's Gin

THE LONDON NO. 1

London, England
www.thelondon1.com

Using a triple distillation method that preserves the botanicals'
infusion until the final step, this artisanal distillation process
is handcrafted by a master distiller and produced
exclusively in small batches.

LABEL:

No. 1 Original Blue Gin

LUCAS BOLS

Amsterdam, Netherlands
www.lucasbols.com

Having started in 1575, Lucas Bols is
the oldest Dutch distillery still active today,
and its brand is synonymous with
quality and innovation.

LABELS:
Bols Genever Gin
Damrak Amsterdam Gin
Bols Silver Top Gin

MAC DONALD DISTILLERY

Snohomish, Washington
www.washingtondistilleries.com

Using ingredients grown entirely in
Washington, this is not a traditional London
dry style gin as it uses notably less juniper
than most gins and emphasizes citrus and
floral notes, making it an American gin.

LABEL:
Isis Premium Gin

MAINE DISTILLERIES, LLC

Freeport, Maine
www.coldrivervodka.com

This gluten-free, gold medal-winning gin (2013 San Francisco World Spirits Competition) is made with farm-grown potatoes and the crisp natural water of Maine's Cold River.

LABEL:

Cold River Traditional Gin

Martin Miller

London, England
www.martinmillersgin.com

Since its 1999 launch this distillery has won numerous international awards from the most respected judges, earning it the distinction of being the most-awarded gin in the Premium and Super Premium categories.

LABELS:
Martin Miller's Gin
Martin Miller's Westbourne Strength

Martin Ryan Distilling Company/Bull Run Distillery

Portland, Oregon
www.ariagin.com

This small-batch, handcrafted gin is the result of four years of recipe trial-and-error, with hundreds of test batches that led to the perfectly balanced flavor of the final product, which can be enjoyed straight or in cocktails.

LABEL:

Aria Portland Dry Gin

MASTER OF MALT

Kent, England
www.masterofmalt.com

Formed in 1985, Master of Malt is a major producer and distributor of a variety of spirits, including all of the gin labels noted below that appeal to a wide range of gin lovers.

LABELS:
Origin—Arezzo, Italy
Origin—Meppel, The Netherlands
Origin—Istog, Kosovo
Origin—Veliki Preslav, Bulgaria
Origin—Klanac, Croatia
Origin—Skopje, Macedonia
Origin—Valbone, Albania
Worship Street Whistling Shop Cream Gin
The Spectator Gin
Professor Cornelius Ampleforth's Bathtub Gin
Professor Cornelius Ampleforth's Bathtub Gin Navy-Strength
Professor Cornelius Ampleforth's Sloe Gin
Professor Cornelius Ampleforth's Old Tom Gin
Professor Cornelius Ampleforth's Cask-Aged Gin
Professor Cornelius Ampleforth's Cask-Aged Navy-Strength Gin

THE MELBOURNE GIN COMPANY

Gembrook, Australia

www.melbournegincompany.com

This maker distills in small batches, using handcraft methods, and employing a non-chill filtering system.

LABEL:

The Melbourne Gin Company Dry Gin

MIKKELLER SPIRITS

Copenhagen, Denmark
www.mikkellerspirits.dk

This high-quality gin is handcrafted in
a small copper pot still in small batches.
In addition to the carefully selected botanicals
mix, the distillery imports US Simcoe hops
to create a smooth sip.

LABEL:
Mikkeller Botanical Gin

MILE HIGH SPIRITS

Denver, Colorado
www.drinkmilehighspirits.com

Mile High is not only a distillery but also
a cocktail lounge and music venue where
patrons are invited to come hang out
and sample its products in a variety
of unique cocktails.

LABEL:
Denver Dry Gin

MONOPOLOWA

Vienna, Austria
www.monopolowa.at

Originally founded in the seventeenth century, Monopolowa's gins have won numerous international awards including the 2013 World Spirits Award gold medal for its eponymous label.

LABELS:
Vienna Dry Gin
Monopolowa Dry Gin

MOONSHINE KID

London, England
www.moonshinekid.com

Moonshine Kid is born from a hip, young, rebellious distillery in downtown London that focuses on handcraft production along with fostering an image of bucking trends and taking risks.

LABEL:
Moonshine Kid Dogs Nose Dry Hop Gin

NEW COLUMBIA DISTILLERS

WASHINGTON, DC
WWW.GREENHATGIN.COM

LABELS:
Green Hat Gin
Seasonal & Aged Variations

The story behind the name Green Hat is a good one, and it is the perfect moniker for a distillery that had the know-how to get DC law changed in order to become the District's first post-Prohibition distillery to legally offer onsite retail and free tastings to the public. Upon arriving in DC, I walk down Fenwick Street and come to a large room, open to me on the street, like a garage—but this is no garage. The interior is vast, clean and mechanically inviting as I approach. New Columbia Distillers is a family operation, owned by Michael Lowe and his wife Melissa Kroning, their daughter Elizabeth Lowe, and her husband John Uselton.

As I enter, Michael and John greet me. I smile and cannot help but look up to view the beautiful towering still. Two rising columns lined with portholes reach at least twenty feet into the air standing next to a large pot still, which resembles some sort of robot from a 1950s science fiction movie. Nick Haase, who works for historic German manufacturer CARL Artisan Distilleries and Brewing Systems (est. 1869), designed the striking still for New Columbia. Other sections of the room are occupied with a mash tun (used to convert grains' starches into sugars for fermentation), hot water tanks, various plumbing and piping, and fermenters.

> "When we learned about 'The Man in the Green Hat,' we knew we had the perfect Washington story for our brand."

In front of me at a tasting station lie containers of each botanical in the Green Hat recipe: coriander seed, fennel seed, cinnamon, orris root, grains of paradise, celery seed, angelica root, lemon grass and sage leaf. In the back, huge sacks of fresh grain are delivered regularly to distill their own in-house base spirit. I ask Michael, "Both of you seem passionate about gin. Has gin always been a shared joy between the two of you?" He replies, "It's a passion that has grown over the last few years as we each started building collections of gin at home and exploring classic gin cocktails. John has about forty gins; I've only got twenty."

"So, it's been a process," I say and ask, "How did the idea to start a distillery evolve?" Lowe answers, "When we learned that it was possible to open up small distillery, we started doing research and got more excited the more we learned. While we were starting our company and looking for a suitable building, we signed up for an excellent apprenticeship at Dry Fly Distilling in Spokane, Washington. That convinced us that it was doable, so we started ordering equipment and locked in our location. It took another year to get our construction done, equipment in place, and all the regulatory approvals."

One aspect of the gin world I have wanted to ask about for a while is the marketing angle. I have seen so many beautiful and diverse bottles and labels, some hand placed, some hand numbered. It is obvious that many craft distillers put a lot of thought and time into the image associated with their spirit. The Green Hat label features a stunning rectangular design that is an aesthetic throwback to Prohibition-era America, with bold stamp-like lettering stating "EVERY MAN HAS HIS VICE." It bares the recognizable logo—a hat—and is hand numbered.

I ask about the label. "Your logo and bottle definitely stand out. What was the process for coming up with your brand and marketing? Your name's origin is explained in detail on your website, but what led you to that?" Lowe explains, "First, we knew we needed a story. We did a lot of research into the history of spirits and distilling in DC. When we learned about 'The Man in the Green Hat,' we knew we had the perfect Washington story for our brand. Then we found an outstanding design team at Design Army in DC. We discussed with them the Green Hat story and what we had in mind for our products over time. They then came up with ten possible label designs for the bottle they agreed we should use. We selected one for our gins and reserved a couple more for additional products. Design Army then built our website and the rest of our branding based on the label design. They did remarkable work."

Although readily available on New Columbia's website, I will briefly describe the tale of "The Man in the Green Hat." Returning from World War I to DC, George Cassiday began a career supplying illegal bootleg booze to many of our nation's finest government officials during Prohibition. He wore a prominent green hat for which he was notoriously dubbed, "The Man in the Green Hat." He was arrested several times—always with his green hat—which seems to have heightened his fame, but does not appear to have spent any time in jail. Could his fortune

in remaining free be perhaps owed to his friends in the House and Senate? A DC Prohibition legacy, Cassiday's situation illustrates just how corrupt lawmakers in power can be, banning a substance publicly while enjoying it within closed circles.

I ask if New Columbia had such luck with DC law, and Lowe tells me, "It took us about nine months to get DC law changed to allow us to sell retail and provide free tastings at the distillery. This involved writing the legislation we needed, dozens of meetings with city council members and their staffs, and ultimately employing a lawyer with experience at the council. We think it took so long to get attention because we were the only distillery and could not promise large employment numbers."

At this point I turn to a machine I've never seen before, kind of like a section of a metallic salad bar with symmetrical purple nozzles hanging down along either side. "What is this?" I ask Michael. "It's a gin cow. We use it for our bottling parties," Michael says, referring to New Columbia's idea to get people in their distillery and get them interested in the spirits community and actually involved in the production process. It's a great idea, and I ask Michael to tell me more about it. "Our bottling parties are great fun for our volunteers. They are usually Saturday afternoons when the distillery is buzzing with visitors here for tastings, tours, and sales. The bottling party is usually twelve to fourteen people—friends, work colleagues, birthday parties, etc. They get the special experience of labeling bottles and filling them with gin for about two hours. They get a detailed tour and their 'tastes' come in the form of custom-made gin and tonics. They also get a discount on any gin they might purchase. We've had a number of people come back for repeat bottlings."

Green Hat gin has been a big hit with DC bars and the drinking public, and its reach is growing as the bottles venture out into surrounding states. They seem to enjoy being in a progressive state of experimentation and do not offer just one product—they also produce seasonal small-batch varieties that come and go. I notice four barrels with a bright company logo stamped on the face. They look so much like art that I wasn't sure if they had a purpose. It turns out the team is also working on a barrel-aged limited-production batch of gin. We sample all three of their current gins, including the barrel-aged right from the barrel, which I thoroughly enjoy. I thank the team for their hospitality and am on my way.

New Deal Distillery

Portland, Oregon
www.newdealdistillery.com

These craft-distilled spirits are inspired by the DIY spirit
of Portland, and the distillery ordered a custom-designed still
that pulls oils, tannins, and heavier elements from
the botanicals during distillation.

LABELS:
New Deal Gin No. 1
Portland Dry Gin Recipe 33

NEW YORK DISTILLING COMPANY

Brooklyn, New York
www.nydistilling.com

Former Brooklyn Brewery cofounder Tom Potter joined with former
Slow Food USA chairman Allen Katz to build this world-class
distillery from scratch in a bare-bones warehouse in Brooklyn.

LABELS:
Dorothy Parker American Gin
Perry's Tot-Navy Strength Gin
Chief Gowanus New-Netherland Gin

NOLET'S

Schiedam, Netherlands
www.noletsgin.com

Handcrafted in Holland behind 300 years' worth of experience by the Nolet family, this distiller produced a short film romanticizing the creation of its spirits, which is available to view on its website.

LABELS:
Nolet's Silver Dry Gin
Nolet's Reserve Dry Gin
Nolet Heritage Prize Medal Geneva

NORTH SHORE DISTILLERY, LLC

Chicago, Illinois
www.northshoredistillery.com

Opened in 2004, this award-winning producer makes distinctive spirits for the modern connoisseur, with each bottle being handmade in small batches.

LABELS:
Distiller's Gin No. 6 Modern Dry Gin
Distiller's Gin No. 11 Classic Dry Gin

NUMBER ZERO DRINKS S.L.

Bordeaux, France
www.number-0.com

The secret ingredient in this gin is the cinchona cuttings
gathered by hand from the Inca Trail in Peru,
where cinchona was first discovered, and which
inspires the distillery to honor the Incan philosophy
of working for and toward nature.

LABEL:

No. 0 London Dry Gin

OLD ST. ANDREWS

Kent, England
www.osawhisky.com

Old St. Andrews' gins have won nearly 20 European spirits awards since hitting the market in 2007. The Pink 47 and London 47 labels are actually the exact same gin—the only difference is that the London 47 label is made for the American market.

LABELS:
Pink 47
London 40
London 47

OLIVER TWIST LONDON DISTILLED

London, England
www.olivertwistgin.com

Traditionally authentic distillation methods are employed in this distillery located on the River Thames in London, and all botanicals are gathered from the Mediterranean region.

LABEL:
Oliver Twist London Distilled Dry Gin

ONDER DE BOOMPJES

Schiedam, South Holland, Netherlands
www.onderdeboompjes.eu

The legacy of this distillery dates back to 1658 when they began making Dutch gin, and continues today with its commitment to using only natural ingredients and handmade, hand-bottled products.

LABELS:
Sylvius Gin
Boompies Premium Genever
Boompies Old Dutch Genever

OOLA DISTILLERY

Seattle, Washington
www.ooladistillery.com

Producing only small batches at a time, this distributor is all about the grain-to-glass craft method that includes a sense of place and connection to the people who grow the ingredients and the distillers who create the final product.

LABEL:
Oola Gin

THE ORGANIC SPIRIT CO.

Bramley, England
www.junipergreen.org

Known as the world's first all-organic London dry gin, the families behind this distillery have over 300 years of experience crafting premium quality spirits with a focus on environmentally sound production.

LABEL:

Juniper Green Organic Gin

PACIFIC DISTILLERY

Woodinville, Washington
www.pacificdistillery.com

This small-batch distiller uses only organically grown botanicals from around the world to distill its ultra-premium spirit in a hand-hammered copper alembic pot still.

LABEL:
Voyager Gin

PARK PLACE DRINKS LTD.

Clackmannanshire, England
www.sw4gin.com

Although this craft distiller discloses each of the 12 botanicals it uses to create its multiple awards-winning gin—see the list on its website—they keep the amounts and methods employed in infusing those botanicals a secret.

LABEL:
SW4 Gin

PEARL SPIRITS

Alberta, Canada
www.pearl-gin.com

First launched in 1999, Pearl gin starts with crisp clean water from Canadian Rocky Mountain streams and gets its alcohol from soft winter wheat grown on the Canadian plains to create a traditional London style gin.

LABEL:
Pearl Gin

PENDERYN DISTILLERY

Penderyn, Wales
www.welsh-whisky.co.uk

Using naturally fresh water from Brecon Beacons National Park and botanicals from the four corners of the Earth, this distillery won the Gold Best in Class award at the 2011 International Wine & Spirits Competition.

LABELS:

Brecon Special Reserve Gin
Brecon Botanicals Gin

PERNOD RICARD

Paris, France
Purchase, New York
www.pernod-ricard.com

Pernod-Ricard USA is a leading premium spirits company in America by volume, and its parent company in Paris, France, is the co-leader in spirits and wine production worldwide.

LABELS:
Plymouth Gin
Plymouth Sloe Gin
Plymouth Navy Strength
Seagram's Extra Dry Gin
Seagram's Twisted Gins
Seagram's Gin & Juice (8 varieties)
Seagram's Distiller's Reserve Gin
Beefeater London Dry Gin
Beefeater 24 Gin
Cork Dry Gin

Philadelphia Distilling

Philadelphia, Pennsylvania
www.philadelphiadistilling.com

Distilled in a custom-built, hand-hammered copper pot still, their method of batch distillation calls for extremely slow heating which allows for maximum separation of impurities and results in the purest of alcohols.

LABEL:

Bluecoat American Dry Gin

PORTOBELLO STAR

London, England
www.portobellostarbar.co.uk

If you find yourself in London, you must
indulge in the "Ginstitute" experience at
Portobello Star. You learn in the basement
gin museum, create your own gin in the
upstairs still room, and leave with a bottle
of your own creation which Portobello will
reproduce for you upon request.

LABEL:
Portobello Road No. 171 Gin

PORT STEILACOOM DISTILLERY

Steilacoom, Washington
www.portsteilacoomdistillery.com

This micro-distillery opened in 2012
and produces small-batch releases of its
products, all of which include honey,
a rare ingredient for gin that adds a light
sweetness and smooth finish.

LABEL:
Homeport Gin

THE POSHMAKERS LTD.

London, England

www.ishgin.com

These handcrafted gins are distilled in a traditional pot still in the heart of London using 12 ingredients in the botanical profile, each of which is macerated for 24 hours before distilling begins to encourage its expression.

LABELS:

Ish London Dry Gin
Ish Limed Gin

PREMIUM DISTILLERY, SL

Cervera, Spain
www.ginebradragons.com

Using botanicals collected in the Pyrenees Mountains, their gins are produced in traditional pot stills and presented in lots of 600 numbered bottles.

LABELS:

Gin Port of Dragons 100% Pure Gin
Gin Port of Dragons 100% Dry Gin
Gin Port of Dragons 100% Floral Gin

PROXIMO SPIRITS

Jersey City, New Jersey
www.proximospirits.com

Known for its floral nose, Boodles was given an "Exceptional" rating by the Beverage Tasting Institute in 2013 and won a silver medal in the 2013 San Francisco World Spirits Competition.

LABEL:

Boodles British Gin

RAFF DISTILLERIE

San Francisco, California
www.raffdistillerie.com

Named after two famous San Francisco dogs from the nineteenth century (google them for a good story), this gin starts as a brandy made from California grapes, then is redistilled using a citrus-focused botanical profile.

LABEL:
Bummer and Lazarus Small Batch Gin

Ransom Spirits

Sheridan, Oregon
www.ransomspirits.com

This artisan producer of small-batch products has won numerous medals, including the 2013 Gold Medal in the San Francisco World Spirits Competition for its Old Tom gin.

LABELS:
Ransom Old Tom Gin
Smalls Gin

Revolution Spirits

Austin, Texas
www.revolutionspirits.com

This small, six-person operation opened in 2014 and focuses on using nothing but all-natural ingredients and handcrafting their spirit through every step of the distilling process.

LABEL:
Austin Reserve Gin

ROGUE DISTILLERY

Portland, Oregon
www.rogue.com

This craft distiller's commitment to growing, malting, roasting, and smoking its own grains and botanicals is one of the reasons it was named the 2014 Distiller of the Year by the World Beverage Competition.

LABEL:
Rogue Spruce Gin

ROYAL DIRKZWAGER DISTILLERIES

Schiedam, The Netherlands
www.vangoghvodka.com

A virtual United Nations of botanicals, this gin includes coriander and licorice from the Middle East, grains of paradise from West Africa, juniper berries from the Netherlands, almonds from Spain, lemons from the United States, and other items from around the world.

LABEL:
Van Gogh Gin

Sacred Distillery

LONDON, ENGLAND
WWW.SACREDSPIRITSCOMPANY.COM

LABELS
Sacred Gin
Pink Grapefruit Gin
Cardamom Gin
Juniper Gin
Coriander Gin
Orris Gin
Licorice Gin

Ian Hart does not merely live in his London home. Within the walls of his Highgate residence, Hart, alongside business partner Hilary Whitney, distills his label of gin, Sacred. It is a true London dry, distilled within the city limits. The kitchen, or what I assume was once the kitchen,

Ian Hart's unique home distillery.

does not look like a kitchen at all but a brilliant chemist's lab. Beakers and condensers, fresh botanicals anticipating their turn, and stacked boxes of bottled finished product fill the room. Bubbling liquids convert into stimulated vapor that will be cooled and collected as a purified seasoned alcohol, all connected by a network of tubing, creating Hart's custom pressurized low-heat still. And Sacred gin is not made in a pot or column still but in glassware.

Hart, who had successful stints on Wall Street and as a London city headhunter, decided to follow a passion, and after relinquishing himself from the business sphere, ventured into the world of wine and then gin in 2008. I ask Hart how he came to have a distillery in his home. He explains that, "It was less expensive as a startup, and to not pay the rent basically. We were kind of surprised to be given the customs

"No one ever said, 'Hey, you can't have a distillery in your home!' Nobody ever said that to us."

and excise distilling licenses and yet they came through the mail, free of charge, in seven days. Not a problem. For some of the more complicated licenses, they came and visited and that was fine. No one ever said, 'Hey, you can't have a distillery in your home!' Nobody ever said that to us."

Hart began experimenting with wine, removing the water and purifying it utilizing a vacuum-sealed still consisting of an array of chemist's glassware. This process took less sufficient wines and made them into something more pronounced. With great vision Hart set out to craft a truly new gin, something that would stand out in a crowd of voluminous indistinguishable products. He then explains the benefits of using his low-heat vacuum still. "It's more inducive to think fresh cut oranges are much fresher than cooked oranges which become a sort of like a stewed marmalade flavor. Most fruits change. Apples turn to stewed apples. Plums turn to stewed plums. Fresh strawberries turn to strawberry jam, and the flavors continually, across the spectrum of botanicals, do change. Hot distillations versus cold distillation; cold distillation typically you see much fresher, much lusher distillates by comparison with hot distillation, which tends to give you more cooked and more earthy flavors."

After much experimentation and 23 revisions later, Hart had found the unique gin he was seeking, Sacred.

Hart's method produces a distinct gin because his process is unique. He macerates the botanicals in the base spirit and then distills each essence separately. Once he has distilled the concentrates of his individual botanicals, he blends them in appropriate fashion to create Sacred gin. Although the exact recipe for Sacred gin is held in secret, Hart does share that it consists of English grain spirit macerated with twelve botanicals including juniper, cardamom, nutmeg, angelica, fresh orange, lime and lemon cuts, and Boswellia Sacra (aka Hougary Frankincense), the last providing the inspiration for the Sacred name. Hart tells me, "You get a very different kind of gin according to

> "The competition are the big brands. The small guys like us are never going to be more than half of one percent of the market, ever."

what your base spirit is. We use English wheat spirit. It produces a very different style of gin by comparison with, I think, most US craft gins, which are made with corn spirit. All gins have their own recipe. The choice of base spirit is probably the number one choice you have to make and it's incredibly important." Hart continues and provides me with a great perspective from afar: "Most UK gins are in fact made with English wheat spirit or Scottish wheat spirit, rather than corn spirit. I believe the opposite is the case in the US.

Ian Hart.

And I think, my personal feeling, is that's one of the defining differences between US and UK gins."

Sacred Distillery is an example of one of many community-based gin scenes. They produce three vermouths, two of which are exclusively made for Alessandro Palazzi of Dukes Bar. In fact, Sacred's label features Palazzi's martini recipe on the back. When you hold of bottle of Sacred gin in your hands you can feel the love and ambition that went into it, including its bottle design: a beautiful gold and purple label, hand numbered. And that's before you even taste it.

I ask Hart about community versus competition in the market. "The competition are the big brands. The small guys like us are never going to be more than half of one percent of the market, ever. In the UK and other European countries the Bicardis and others will do deals with big bars which are based on quantity breaks, and investments in their materials and special promotions where there's kickbacks and what have you, which make it very difficult for small brands to get any appreciable volume. The real competition is the big brands, and what I'd say is that it's a somewhat anti-competitive axis in the UK, less so perhaps in the US."

Sacred has expanded and also offers London vodka, a spiced English vermouth, and Sacred Rosehip Cup, which may be used in place of Campari in cocktails. They also offer the Sacred Gin Blending Kit that includes separate distillates of each botanical for home blending. Hart says about the kit, "Because we distill all our botanicals separately, we thought it would be fun. In fact one of the reasons we started doing that was because it gives you the opportunity to change your gin blend very quickly in comparison with distilling them all at once. So say this blend doesn't have enough citrus, or maybe it's got too much juniper, for example, you don't have to go back to square one and do the whole distillation again. You just change the proportion of that particular distillate."

Since opening, Sacred gin has ranked at the top in spirits competitions and has international distribution including to the United States. Hart and Whitney exemplify the modern craft mindset where locally produced small-batch products may be enjoyed globally.

SAN JUAN ISLAND DISTILLERY

Friday Harbor, Washington
www.sjidistillery.com

Employing a 30-liter Portuguese pot still just for making gin, this small distillery's spirits owe their unique flavor to the use of San Juan Island's indigenous ingredients, including wild roses, lavender, blackberries, hand-foraged island barks, and other local botanicals.

LABELS:

Spy Hop Gin
Seasonal Spy Hop Gin
Spy Hop Barrel-Aged Gin
Spy Hop Harvest Select Navy Strength Gin

SEATTLE CIDER CO.

Seattle, Washington
www.seattlecidercompany.com

Although they do not make gin, it is appropriate to include this maker here thanks to their unique gin-flavored cider.

LABEL:
Gin Botanical Hard Cider

SEATTLE DISTILLING COMPANY

Southwest Vashon, Washington
www.seattledistillingcompany.com

Vapor-infused botanicals complement the purity of the crisp Cascade Mountains water to create a complex and invigorating gin.

LABEL:
Alpinist Gin

SIPSMITH INDEPENDENT SPIRITS

London, England
www.sipsmith.com

Boasting the first copper distillery in London for 200 years, every production of this artisanal distillery is meticulously researched and handcrafted.

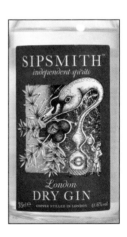

LABELS:
Sipsmith London Dry Gin
Sipsmith Sloe Gin
V.J.O.P. (A Very Junipery Over Proof gin)
Sipsmith Summer Cup

SIR ROBERT BURNETT & CO

Heaven Hill Distillery, Bardstown, Kentucky
www.heavenhill.com

Heaven Hill Distillery is America's largest independent, family-owned producer of distilled spirits.

LABELS:
Sir Robert Burnett's London Dry Gin
Burnett's White Satin (vintage)

Smooth Ambler Spirits Co.

Maxwelton, West Virginia
www.smoothambler.com

Starting with locally sourced botanicals, pure mountain water, and an ideal climate, this craft distiller has a hands-on approach to each step of the process.

LABELS:

Smooth Ambler Greenbrier Gin
Smooth Ambler Barrel Aged Gin

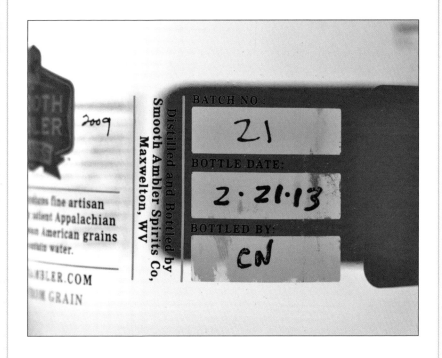

SOUND SPIRITS

Seattle, Washington
www.drinksoundspirits.com

Seattle's first craft distillery to open since Prohibition, their artisan spirits are produced slowly, one batch at a time, with a focus on authentic methods and best ingredients.

LABELS:
Ebb+Flow Gin
Old Tom Gin

Spencerfield Spirit Company

Inverkeithing, England
www.spencerfieldspirit.com

A small-batch gin maker that focuses on packing in the flavors of the finest juniper berries.

LABELS:
Edinburgh Gin
Edinburgh Raspberry Gin Liqueur
Edinburgh Elderflower Gin Liqueur

St. George Spirits

Alameda, California

www.stgeorgespirits.com

As the distillers set out to craft their entry into the delightful category of gin, in the end they decided to make *three* gins to express the various flavor profiles they sought.

LABELS:

St. George Terroir Gin

St. George Botanivore Gin

St. George Dry Rye Gin

THE STING

London, England
www.thestingpremiumgin.com

The Sting uses "batch distillation" that does not mix various distillations, therefore creating a purer and more quality-controlled bottle.

LABEL:

The Sting Small Batch London Dry Gin

SUN LIQUOR DISTILLERY

Seattle, Washington
www.sunliquor.com

Their gins are twice-distilled, slowly, in copper pot stills and rested in stainless steel before bottling. Winners of a gold medal at the San Francisco World Spirits Competition in 2012.

LABELS:

Hedge Trimmer Gin
Gun Club Gin

SUPERIOR PREMIUM SPIRITS

Loveland, Colorado
www.spring44.com

This craft distiller started by two local friends relies on pure Rocky Mountain water from the natural spring that is its namesake.

LABEL:
Spring 44 Gin

TAILOR MADE SPIRITS COMPANY

Gidgegannup, Western Australia

www.thewestwindsgin.com

This craft distiller uses exotic Western Australian ingredients—including the likes of wattle seed and bush tomato—to create these two one-of-a-kind gins.

LABELS:

The West Winds Cutlass Gin

The West Winds Sabre Gin

THAMES DISTILLERS

London, England
www.fiftypoundsgin.co.uk

Genuine English small-batch gin production where carefully selected ingredients ensure a strikingly smooth London dry gin.

LABEL:

Fifty Pounds Gin

TOORANK DISTILLERIES

Zevenaar, Netherlands

www.sloanes-gin.com

Hailing from the land of gin's birth, this label won World's Best Gin and a double gold medal at the San Francisco World Spirits Competition in 2011.

LABEL:

Sloane's Gin

TREATY OAK DISTILLING

Austin, Texas
www.treatyoakrum.com

A craft-distilled and uniquely Texas-inspired gin featuring botanicals local to the Lone Star State; it's inspired a number of famous local cocktails in the state capital.

LABELS:
Waterloo Gin
Waterloo Barrel-Aged Gin

VALTVODKA
COMPANY LTD.

Paisley, Scotland
www.valtvodka.com

Gilt has produced this fine single-malt gin, distilled five times from malted barley at a sole Scottish distillery.

LABEL:
Gilt Single Malt Scottish Gin

VENUS SPIRITS

Santa Cruz, California
www.venusspirits.com

Small craft distillery creates this micro-batched gin with classic flavor profiles.

LABEL:
Venus Gin

VIKRE DISTILLERY

Duluth, Minnesota
www.vikredistillery.com

The pristine beauty of Lake Superior, the North Woods, and
the boundary waters of Minnesota are infused into the products
made by three families who emigrated from Norway and
whose name means, "people of the bay."

LABELS:
Boreal Spruce
Boreal Juniper
Boreal Cedar

W.J. Stillman Ltd.

London, England

This label is produced for and exported to Trader Joe's in the US by a distillery in England.

LABEL:

Rear Admiral Joseph's London Original Dry Gin

Wemyss Vintage Malts Ltd.

Edinburgh, Scotland
www.wemyssmalts.com

This traditional Scottish distiller (pronounced "Weems") has been producing fine spirits since the nineteenth century.

LABELS:

Darnley's View Gin
Darnley's View Spiced Gin

WEST END DRINKS

London, England
www.kingofsohogin.com

Distilled in the heart of London and embodying the characteristics that make Soho unique, this label has a unique flavor profile featuring 12 botanicals.

LABEL:
The King of Soho Gin

WHITLEY NEILL LIMITED

London, England
www.whitleyneill.com

Distilled in small batches by a direct descendant of Thomas Greenall and a long line of distillers, this handcraft gin's flavor profile is inspired by the beauty and mystery of Africa.

LABEL:
Whitley Neill London Dry

WISHKAH RIVER DISTILLERY

Aberdeen, Washington
www.wishkahriver.com

Award-winning craft distiller in the southwest corner of
the state offers unconventional gin that features
a proprietary juniper-botanical mix.

LABEL:
Bulfinch 83 Unfiltered Gin

XORIGUER

Mahón-Menorca, Spain
www.xoriguer.es

Produced by an influential family with centuries-old roots
on the Spanish island, Xoriguer has been denominated
a "guaranteed traditional specialty."

LABEL:
Xorigeur Gin, Gin De Mahon

ZEPHYR
IMPORTS

Carlsbad, California
www.zephyrgin.com

Infused with elderberry and gardenia to create a smooth, premium English gin.

LABEL:
Zephyr Gin

ZUIDAM
DISTILLERS

Baarle-Nassau, Netherlands
www.zuidam.eu

A family owned and operated artisanal distillery whose recipes are all created by the father-and-son team using all natural ingredients.

LABEL:
Zuidam Genever

ACKNOWLEDGMENTS

Thank you most of all to my loving and supportive wife, Katie Barbato, who drank gin with me on many nights and in many cities.

Thank you to all the people who took the time to discuss gin with me and reveal where gin has been and where it's going, and to all who showed me hospitality and kindness throughout my travels. Buz & Janet Teacher, Ben Koenig, Mary Ann & Richard Koenig, Mike & Randi Lawson, Taylor Kogut, John Whalen, Greg Jones, Carlo DeVito, John Whalen III, Clare Pelino, Whitney Cookman, Ben & Sarah Johnson, Phil Palazzolo, Dre Mazzenga & Tracy Sampedro, Katie Avery, Lauren Olivia Ruffin, Alex Atwood & Nupur Pandey, Michelle Lewis, David Schlessinger, Guli Fager, Rob Barbato & Navassa Hilbertz, John & Susan Barbato, Keanan McCabe & CarrieLee Anderson, Obie & Denise O'Brien, Greg Pechetti, Sarah Lockwood, Katie Loeb, Sarah Bonkowski & James Hearne, Adam & Lindsay Schwartz, Matthew & Rebecca Rankin, Steven Renzi, Nick & Diane Williams, Derek Smock, Noah Horton, Ron Bauman, Melissa Cookman, Michael Nuceder, Stephen René Poteau, Julia Forte, N.A. Poe, Derek Brown, Erik Holzherr, Frank Cisneros, Arrigo Cipriani, Jason Stevens, Rob Pate, Neil Kopplin, Steven DeAngelo, Ryan Mararian & Christian Krogstad, Michael Lowe, John Ludin, Ian Hart, Mike Groener, and everyone else who took time to discover the spirit of gin with me.

SOURCES

BOOKS

Baker Jr., Charles H., *The Gentleman's Companion, Volume II: Being an Exotic Drinking Book*, Crown Publishers, New York, NY, 1946

Barnett, Richard, *The Book of Gin*, Grove Press, New York, NY, 2011

Coates, Geraldine, *The Mixellany Guide to Gin*, Mixellany Books, Cheltenham, UK, 2012

Degroff, Dale, *The Essential Cocktail: The Art of Mixing Perfect Drinks*, Clarkson Potter, New York, NY, 2008

Emerson, Edward R., *Beverages, Past and Present*, G.P. Putnam's Sons, New York, NY, 1908

"Jimmy," *Cocktails: by "Jimmy" Late of Ciro's London*, David McKay Company, Philadelphia, PA, 1933

Okrent, Daniel, *Last Call: The Rise and Fall of Prohibition*, Scribner, New York, NY, 2010

Parsons, Brad Thomas, *Bitters: A Spirited History of a Classic Cure-All*, Ten Speed Press, Berkeley, CA, 2011

Solmonson, Lesley Jacobs, *Gin: A Global History*, Reaktion Books, London, England, 2012

Stewart, Amy, *The Drunken Botanist: The Plants That Create the World's Great Drinks*, Algonquin Books of Chapel Hill, Chapel Hill, NC, 2013

Wondrich, David, *Imbibe*, Penguin Group USA, New York, NY, 2007

WEBSITES

www.12bottlebar.com

www.brewwiki.com

www.drinks.seriouseats.com

www.esquire.com

www.foodandwine.com

www.ginreviews.com

www.gintender.com

www.gintime.com

www.homemadegin.com

www.imbibemagazine.com

www.martiniwarehouse.com

www.npr.com

www.nytimes.com

www.pbs.org

prohibition.osu.edu

www.reclaimingprovincial.com

www.summerfruitcup.wordpress.com

www.theginisin.com

ONLINE ARTICLES

Gray, Kevin, "Corpse Reviver #2," September 14, 2009, http://cocktailenthusiast.com/corpse-reviver-2

Greene, Phil, "The Hemingway Gin and Tonic," March 20, 2007, http://cocktailmuseum.wordpress.com/2007/03/20/the-hemingway-gin-and-tonic/

Hamlin, Matt, "Hemingway's Green Isaacs Special," December 12, 2011, http://ajiggerofblog.com/2011/12/12/hemingways-green-isaacs-special/

O'Ceallaigh, John, "London's gin palaces, past and present," March 21, 2013, http://www.telegraph.co.uk/luxury/travel/1255/londons-gin-palaces-past-and-present.html

Romine, Andy, "Booze Nerd: The Corpse Reviver #2," February 4, 2011, http://functionalnerds.com/2011/02/booze-nerd-the-corpse-reviver-2/

Sinclair, George, "Tom Collins Article," March 26, 2007, http://www.scribd.com/doc/18790/Tom-Collins-Article

Willett, Megan, "The Weird Story of How the Tom Collins Cocktail Got Its Name," July 17, 2013, http://www.businessinsider.com/how-the-tom-collins-got-its-name-2013-7

INDEX

ice cubes, 198
ice scoop, 204
ice variations, 197–200
Iceberg, St. John's, Canada, 292
Imbibe, 361
Imbue Cellars, Gaston, Oregon, 163–64
Indio Spirits, Portland, Oregon, 292
Intl. Beverage Holdings Ltd., USA., Inc., New York, 293
Islands in the Stream, 64, 139
It's 5 Artisan Distillery, Cashmere, Washington, 294

jasmine, 185
jigger, 205
Jonge Genever (young style), 86
juniper berries, 11, 29, 31, 184

Knockeen Hills, Canterbury, England, 295
Koenig, Ben, 161–62
Korenwsijn (grain wine), 86

Langley's, Hampshire, England, 296
Langtons of Skiddaw, Lakeland, England, 296
Lark Distillery, Tasmania, Australia, 297
Last Call: The Rise and Fall of Prohibition, 361
lavender, 185
lemon, 188–90
Letherbee Distillers, Chicago, 298
Liberty Party, 47
Little Bird, London, 299
London dry gin, 92
London Gin Club, 17
London Gin Craze, 28
London Gin Palaces, 37, 40
loopholes during Prohibition, 52
Lucas Bols, Amsterdam, Netherlands, 302

Mac Donald Distillery, Snohomish, Washington, 302
"Madame Geneva," 25
Maine Distilleries, Freeport, Maine, 303
Martin Miller, London, 304
Martin Ryan Distilling Company/Bull Run Distillery, Portland, Oregon, 305
martini glass, 204
Martini, 119
martini, precursors to, 134
Master of Malt, Kent, England, 306
medicinal alcohol, 52
Melbourne Gin Company, Gembrook, Australia, 307
MI5, 44
Mikkeller Spirits, Copenhagen, Denmark, 308
Mile High Spirits, Denver, Colorado, 309
Mixellany Guide to Gin, The, 361
mixing glass, 205
Mockingbird Hill, Washington, DC, 42

Monopolowa, Vienna, Austria, 309
Moonshine Kid, London, 309
muddler, 205

Navy strength gin, 104
Negroni, 106
New American dry gin, 92–94
New Columbia Distillers, Washington, DC, 310–13
New Deal Distillery, Portland, Oregon, 314
New York Distilling Company, Brooklyn, 315
No. 209 Aviation, 84
Nolet's, Schiedam, Netherlands, 316
North Shore Distillery, LLC, Chicago, 317
Number Zero Drinks S.L., Bordeaux, France, 318

O.H. Byron's 1884 Martinez, 121
Old St. Andrews, Kent, England, 319
Old Tom gin, 87–92
Oliver Twist London Distilled, London, 320
Onder de Boompjes, Schiedam, South Holland, Netherlands, 320
one-shot and two-shot distillation methods, 103
Oola Distillery, Seattle, Washington, 321
Organic Spirit Company, Bramley, England, 322
orris root, 185
Oude Genever (old style), 86

Pacific Distillery, Woodinville, Washington, 323
Park Place Drinks Ltd., Clackmannanshire, England, 323
Pearl Spirits, Alberta, Canada, 324
Peché, Austin, Texas, 105–8
Penderyn Distillery, Penderyn, Wales, 325
Pernod Ricard, Paris, 326
Peru Club, 80–84
Philadelphia Distilling, Philadelphia, Pennsylvania, 327
Philadelphia, 174–78
Pimm's No. 1 Fruit Cup, 104
Pink Lady, 139
Pistachio Gin Fizz, 195
Plymouth gin, 104
Poe, N.a., 53–54
Police And Thieves, 42
Port Steilacoom Distillery, Steilacoom, Washington, 328
Portobello Star, London, 328
Poshmakers Ltd., London, 329
pot-distilled gin, 78–79
Premium Distillery, SL, Cervera, Spain, 330
Prohibition, 25, 28, 47–49, 311–12
Proximo Spirits, Jersey City, New Jersey, 330

Raff Distillerie, San Francisco, 331
Ransom Spirits, Sheridan, Oregon, 332

ART CREDITS

ABOUT THE AUTHOR

Matt Teacher is the author of fourteen books and journals including *The Home Distiller's Handbook* and *The Little Pink Book of Cocktails* (both by Cider Mill Press). He has worked in the entertainment industry for more than fifteen years, and opened Sine Studios in 2006, collaborating with artists such as Bon Jovi, Bonnie Prince Billy, Natasha Bedingfield, the Fray, and more. He lives in Philadelphia, PA.

ABOUT THE FOREWORD AUTHOR

Arrigo Cipriani was born just one year after his father, Giuseppe, opened Harry's Bar in Venice, Italy. Mr. Cipriani has made it his life's work to continue the family tradition of being a leading force in cocktail culture. Long frequented by famous people—from Ernest Hemingway to Woody Allen—Harry's Bar was declared a national landmark in 2001.